CBSE Term II
2022

Political Science

Class XI

CBSE Term II
2022

Political Science

Class XI

- Complete Theory Covering NCERT
- Case Based Questions
- Short/Long Answer Type Questions
- 3 Practice Papers with Explanations

Author
Shubhendra Tiwari

ARIHANT PRAKASHAN (School Division Series)

ARIHANT PRAKASHAN (School Division Series)

 **Administrative & Production Offices**

Regd. Office
'Ramchhaya' 4577/15, Agarwal Road, Darya Ganj, New Delhi -110002
Tele: 011- 47630600, 43518550

卐 **Head Office**
Kalindi, TP Nagar, Meerut (UP) - 250002, Tel: 0121-7156203, 7156204

卐 **Sales & Support Offices**
Agra, Ahmedabad, Bengaluru, Bareilly, Chennai, Delhi, Guwahati, Hyderabad, Jaipur, Jhansi, Kolkata, Lucknow, Nagpur & Pune.

卐 **ISBN :** 978-93-25796-80-5

PO No : TXT-XX-XXXXXXX-X-XX

Published by Arihant Publications (India) Ltd.

For further information about the books published by Arihant, log on to www.arihantbooks.com or e-mail at info@arihantbooks.com

Follow us on   

Contents

Watch Free Learning Videos

Subscribe **arihant** You**Tube** Channel

☑ Video Solutions of CBSE Sample Papers
☑ Chapterwise Important MCQs
☑ CBSE Updates

Syllabus

CBSE Term II Class XI

Units	Contents	Weightage (in Marks)
PART A : Indian Constitution at Work		
1.	Legislature	07
2.	Executive	07
3.	Judiciary	06
PART B : Political Theory		
1.	Liberty	07
2.	Equality	07
3.	Justice	06
	Total	**40**

CHAPTER 01

Legislature

In this Chapter...

- Introduction
- Need of the Parliament
- Need for Two Houses of Parliament
- Functions of the Parliament

Introduction

The law making body of the government is known as **legislature**. Legislature is the highest deliberative organ in a democracy. It is the body which helps in making represent alines responsible to the people. This makes legislature efficient and effective. Legislatures are elected by the people and work on behalf of the people.

Legislature involve in action such as walkouts, protests, demonstrations, consensus, concern and co-operation. All of these are really important. Without a representative, efficient, and successful legislature, a true democracy is unthinkable. This is the foundation of representative democracy. Legislature is recognised as one of the most democratic and open forum for debate where the executive is answerable to the legislature.

Need of the Parliament

Need for Parliament arises due to the following reasons

- It is a legislative organ of the governemnt. It enables citizens of India to participate in decision making and control the government.
- It contributes to the legislative process and, from time to time introduces new legislation.
- It maintains financial control over the government's revenue, i.e. the government cannot spend public funds without Parliament's permission.

- It is in charge of the government's executive branch. This means that in order for the organ to function, it must have a mandate from Parliament.

Need for Two Houses of Parliament

The **National legislature** is referred to as Parliament. **State Legislature** is the name given to the legislature of each state. Indian Parliament is divided into two houses the Council of States or **Rajya Sabha** and the House of the People or **Lok Sabha.** State Legislature is also divided into two Houses, **Legislative Council** and **Legislative Assembly**.

Rajya Sabha

Rajya Sabha represents the States of India to the Parliament. Its members are indirectly elected by the elected members of the **State Legislative Assembly**. Representation of seats to the second chamber is done according to the size of the population of the states, that means states with large population will have more seats than the states with less population or as a **symmetrical representation**[1].

Representation of Seats

In the USA, every state has equal representation in the Senate. This ensures equality of all the states. But this also means that a small state would have the same representation as the larger states. The system of representation adopted for the Rajya Sabha is different from that in the USA.

---

1. **Symmetrical Representation** It refers to where the members of states in Rajya Sabha are equally represented. They are not elected on the basis of size and population.

The number of members to be elected from each State has been fixed by the Fourth Schedule of the Constitution.

Members of the Rajya Sabha are elected for a term of **six years** and can be re-elected. All members of the Rajya Sabha do not complete their term at the same time. Every two years, **one-third members** of the Rajya Sabha complete their term and elections are held for one-third seats only. Thus, the Rajya Sabha is never dissolved and is called the **permanent House** of the Parliament.

The benefit of this arrangement is that it allows the Rajya Sabha to meet and perform urgent work even if the Lok Sabha has been dissolved and elections have not yet been held. Apart from elected members, Rajya Sabha also has **twelve nominated members** which are nominated by the President, and these nominations are made from among persons who are in the fields of literature, science, art and social service.

Powers of Rajya Sabha

- It considers and approves non-money bill and suggests amendments to money bills.
- It approves constitutional amendments.
- It exercise control over executive by asking questions, introducing motions and resolutions.
- It participate in the elections and removal of the President, Vice-President, Judges of Supreme Court and High Court.
- It can alone initiate the procedure for removal of Vice-President.
- It can give Union Parliament powers to make laws on matters included in the state list.
- The Rajya Sabha is the **representation of states** and its purpose is to protect the powers of states, thus, the Union Parliament needs the approval of the Rajya Sabha to alter the matter prescribed in the State List. This provision adds to the strength of the Rajya Sabha.

Special Powers of Rajya Sabha

- The Rajya Sabha is an **institutional mechanism**[2] to provide representation to the States. Its purpose is to protect the powers of the state. Therefore, any matter that affects the States must be referred to it for its consent and approval. Thus, if the Union Parliament wishes to remove a matter from the State List to either the Union List or Concurrent List in the interest of the country, the approval of Rajya Sabha is necessary.
- The Council of Ministers is responsible to the Lok Sabha and not the Rajya Sabha. As a result, the Rajya Sabha can criticise the government but not overthrow it.

- The Rajya Sabha is elected by MLAs rather than the directly by the public. As a result, the Rajya Sabha was not given certain powers under the constitution. The people are the final authority in a democratic government, as defined by our constitution. According to this argument, the representatives who are directly elected by the people should have the right to remove a government and oversee its finances.
- The powers of the Lok Sabha and Rajya Sabha are co-equal in all other areas, including the passing of non-money bills, constitutional amendments, impeachment of the President and removal of the Vice-President.

Lok Sabha

The Lok Sabha and the State Legislative Assemblies are directly elected by the people on the basis of **Universal Adult Suffrage**, where the value of vote of every individual is equal. The strength of the Lok Sabha is 543.

The members are elected for a period of **five years**. The house can be dissolved if the Prime Minister advices the President to dissolve the House and hold fresh elections, or if no party or coalition can form the government.

Powers of Lok Sabha

- It makes laws on matters included in the Union List and Concurrent List.
- It can introduce and enact money bill and non-money bills.
- It approves proposal for taxation, budgets and annual financial statements.
- It controls the executive by asking questions, supplementary questions, resolutions and motions.
- It amends the constitution.
- It approves the proclamation of Emergency.
- Lok Sabha elects and removes the President, Vice President and removal the judges of Supreme Court and High Court.
- It establishes committees and commissions and considers their reports.

Unicameral/Bicameral Legislature

The legislature of state is known as State Legislature. The constitution has given the states the option of establishing either a **unicameral**[3] or **bicameral legislature**[4]. As of 2021, there are only six states that have a bicameral legislature in India namely, **Andhra Pradesh, Bihar, Karnataka, Maharashtra, Telangana** and **Uttar Pradesh**.

Usually, countries with large size and diversity have bicameral legislature at the centre to give representation to all sections in the society and also to give representation to all geographical regions of the country.

2. **Institutional Mechanism** It refers to the procedures laid down in the constitution for a particular task.

3. **Unicameral Legislature** It is the practice of having a single legislative or parliamentary chamber.

4. **Bicameral Legislature** It is the practice of having two Houses of Parliament.

A Bicameral legislature also serves the advantage to have every decision reconsidered, it means that every bill and policy would be discussed twice and ensures a double check on every matter.

Bicameralism in Germany

Germany has a bicameral legislature. The two Houses are known as **Federal Assembly** (Bundestag) and **Federal Council** (Bundesrat). Assembly is elected by a complex system combining direct and proportional representation for a period of four years.

The 16 federal states of Germany are represented in the Federal Council. These members are generally the ministers in the governments at the state level and are appointed, not elected, by the governments of the federal states.

The Bundesrat does not vote on all legislative initiatives but all the policy areas on which the federal states have concurrent powers and are responsible for federal regulations must be passed by it. It can also veto such legislation.

Functions of the Parliament

Apart from law making, the Parliament is engaged in many other functions, such as

- **Legislative Function** The Parliament is the main law making body in the country. The task of **drafting the bill** is done by the bureaucracy under the supervision of the minister concerned. The substance and timing of the bill are decided by the Cabinet and no major bill is introduced in the Parliament without the approval of the cabinet.

- **Control of Executive and Ensuring its Accountability** The most vital function of the Parliament is to ensure that the executive does not overstep its authority and remains responsible to the people who have elected them.

- **Financial Function** In a democracy, legislature controls taxations and is used by the government. No new tax can be introduced without the approval of Lok Sabha. The financial powers of the Parliament involves the grant of resources to the government to implement its programmes. The government has to give an account to the legislature about the expenditure of money and resources. In order to ensure that the government does not overspend, the **budget** and **annual financial statements** are prepared.

- **Representation** Parliament represents the divergent views of members from different regional, social, economic and religious groups of different parts of the country.

- **Debating Function** The Parliament is the **highest forum of debate** in the country without any limitation on its power of discussion and the members are free to speak on any matter without fear. These discussions constitute the heart of democratic decision-making.

- **Constituent Function** The Parliament has the power to enact changes to the constitution and both the houses are similar in the constituent powers. All the amendments have to be approved by a **special majority** of both the houses.

- **Electoral Functions** The Parliament also performs some electoral functions, as it elects the President and Vice-President of India.

- **Judicial Functions** The judicial functions of the Parliament includes considering the proposals for removal of President, Vice-President and judges of High Courts and Supreme Court. It performs **quasi-judicial** or **semi-judicial functions**[5].

Procedure of Parliament to Make Laws

The basic function of any legislature is to make laws for its people. A definite procedure is followed in the process of making law. Some of the procedure of law making are mentioned in the constitution, which some have evolved from conventions.

A bill is a draft of the proposed law. There can be different types of bills. When a non-minister proposes a bill, it is called **Private Member's Bill**. A bill proposed by a minister is described as **Government Bill**.

Before a bill is introduced in the Parliament, there may be a lot of debate on the need for introducing a bill. The cabinet considers all these debates before arriving at a decision to enact a bill. After the approval from the Cabinet, the task of drafting the legislation begins by the concerned ministry.

The detailed procedure followed by Parliament is given below

- **First Stage** Introduction of a bill in the Parliament constitute the first stage. A bill can either be introduced in the Lok Sabha or Rajya Sabha, except the **money bill** which can only be introduced in Lok Sabha.

- **Second Stage** The bill is sent to committee for recommendation and then sent back to the house. In case of Money Bill. It is introduced in Lok Sabha only. Once passed from Lok Sabha, it is moved to Rajya Sabha. A large part of the discussion on the bills takes place in the committees. The recommendation of the committee is then sent to the House. That is why committees are referred to as **miniature legislatures**.

- **Third Stage** The bill is then voted by the members. If a non-money bill is passed by one house, it is sent to the other house where it goes through the same procedure.

---

5. **Quasi-Judicial** or **Semi-Judicial** These bodies are non-judicial bodies like Commissions or Tribunals which can interpret the law.

- **Final Stage** A bill has to be passed by both the houses for enactment and if there is disagreement between the Houses on the proposed bill, then a joint session of the Parliament is held to resolve the deadlock.

  If it is money bill, the Rajya Sabha may give its suggestion or delay the passage by **14 days** and after that it is deemed to have been passed if no action is taken within 14 days by Rajya Sabha.

- Any amendments suggested by Rajya Sabha may or may not be accepted by the Lok Sabha. When the bill is passed by both the houses, it is sent to the President for his assent. Finally, the assent of the President results in the enactment of bill into a law.

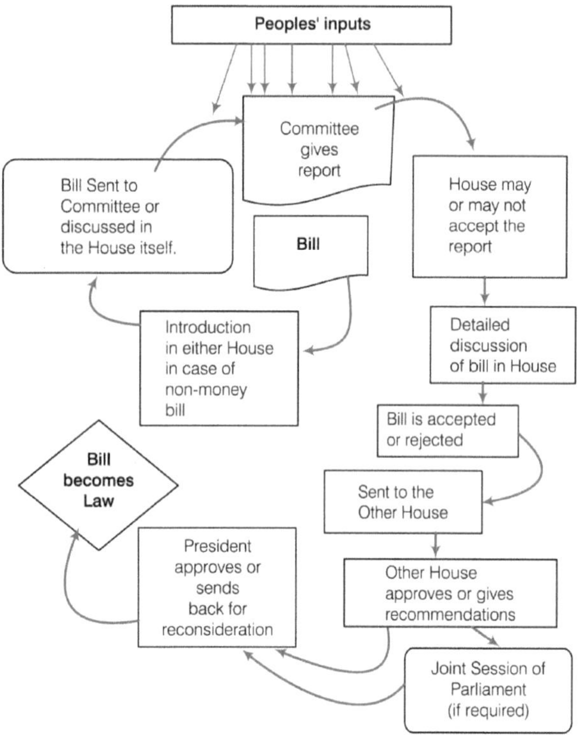

Procedure of Parliament to Make Laws

Parliament Control Over Executive

In order to keep regular and effective check on the executive, the Parliament needs to be active and vigilant in approach. There are many ways of Parliament to control the executive.

Basic to all of them is the power and freedom of the legislators as people's representatives to work effectively and fearlessly.

For example, no action can be initiated against a member of Parliament for whatever said in the legislature because the members have parliamentary privileges. The presiding officer of the legislature has the final powers in deciding matters of breach of privilege. The main purpose of privileges is to enable the members of the legislature to represent the people and exercise effective control over the executive.

Instruments of Parliamentary Control

The legislature in parliamentary system ensures executive accountability during policy making, implementation of law or policy through various devices which are discussed below

Deliberation and Discussion

The members of the legislature get an opportunity to deliberate on the policy direction of the executive and the ways in which policies are implemented during law making process. Apart from deliberating on bills, control may also be exercised during general discussions in the House.

The **Question Hour** is held every day during the sessions of Parliament, where ministers have to respond to questions raised by members.

Zero Hour where members are free to raise any matter that they think is important, half an hour discussion on matters of public importance and adjournment motion are some of the **instruments of exercising control**.

Among the various instruments of exercising control over executive, the question hour is proved to be the most prevalent and effective as the issue of public interest such as price rise, availability of food grains, atrocities on weaker sections, riots, black marketing, etc. are questioned.

Approval and Refusal of Laws

A bill can become a law only after approval of both the Houses of Parliament therefore Parliamentary control is exercised through its **powers of ratification**. A government who has majority in the Lok Sabha but not in Rajya Sabha needs the approval of both the Houses for a bill to become law.

The approvals are the product of intense bargaining and negotiations amongst the members of ruling party or coalition of parties and even between government and opposition.

Financial Control

Financial resources to implement the policies and programmes of the government are granted through the **budget**. Preparation and presentation of budget for the approval of the legislature is the **constitutional obligation** of government. This obligation allows the legislature to exercise control over the purse strings (money power) of the government.

It can enquire into cases of misuse of funds on the basis of the report of the **Comptroller and Auditor General** and **Public Accounts Committees**.

The legislature is concerned about the policies of the government that are reflected in the budget. Through financial control, the legislature controls the policy of government.

No-Confidence Motion

The most powerful weapon that enables the Parliament to ensure executive accountability is the no-confidence motion. The government has to retain the support of the party or coalition to maintain its majority in the Lok Sabha. If a no-confidence motion against the government is passed, the government loses majority. Thus, the Parliament can effectively control the executive and ensures a more responsive government.

As a result, Parliament can exert effective control on the executive and ensure that the administration is more responsive. However, it is critical for this reason that the House has sufficient time at its disposal, that members are interested in discussion and actively participate, and that both the administration and the opposition are willing to compromise.

The number of sessions of the Lok Sabha and State Legislative Assemblies, as well as the amount of time spent debating, has steadily decreased during the previous two decades. Furthermore, the Houses of Parliament have been hampered by a lack of quorum, as well as a boycott of sessions by opposition members, depriving the house of the capacity to regulate the executive through debate.

Parliamentary Committees

The Parliament has appointed various committees for distinct legislative purposes and for day to day business of house. The parliamentary committees performs functions such as study the issue of consideration in legislation, study the demands for grants made by various ministries, expenditure incurred by various departments, investigating the cases of corruption, etc.

Since 1983, India has developed a system of **Parliamentary Standing Committees** to supervise the work of various departments, their budgets, expenditure and bills that come up in the house relating to department.

Joint Parliamentary Committees are set up for the purpose of discussing a particular bill or investigating financial irregularities. Members of these committees are selected from both the houses. The committee system have occupied a position of eminence in our country and has reduced the burden on the Parliament, as many important bills have been referred to committees. No bill can become law and no budget will be sanctioned unless approved by the Parliament but it has been viewed that the Parliament rarely rejects the suggestions made by the committees.

Regulation of the Parliament

Parliament is the **forum of debate** and through its debate Parliament performs all its vital functions. Such discussions must be meaningful and orderly to carry out the functions of the Parliament smoothly. The constitution has made certain provisions to ensure smooth conduct of business and made the **presiding officer**, the final authority in regulating the business of the legislature.

Furthermore, another way to control the behaviour of the member by the presiding officer is, **anti-defection law**, which means that a legislator who is elected on one party's ticket is restricted from defecting to another party.

The presiding officer of the House is the authority who takes final decisions on all such cases.

If it is proved that a member has **defected**, then such member loses the membership of the House. Besides, such a person is also disqualified from holding any political office like ministership, etc.

Defection occurs when a member fails to appear in the House when asked by the party leadership to do so, votes against the party's instructions or willingly departs the party's membership.

Parliamentary Officials

Speaker

In our parliamentary democracy, the Speaker's Office plays a critical role. The Speaker's Office has been defined as representing the full authority of the House of Commons, while members of Parliament represent individual constituencies. Speakers serve from the date of their election until the first meeting of the Lok Sabha after the dissolution of the one to which they were elected.

He or she is eligible for re-election. The Speaker's position is a constitutional one. The Speaker is bound by the provisions of the Constitution as well as the Rules of Procedure and Conduct of Business in Lok Sabha.

While the Speaker ceases to be a member of the House when the Lok Sabha is dissolved, he or she does not vacate his or her office. The Speaker can resign at any time by writing to the Deputy Speaker under his or her hand.

Speaker of the Lok Sabha can be removed by the Lok Sabha by a resolution passed by an effective majority (more than 50% of the total strength excluding vacancies) of the House.

The Speaker and Deputy Speaker of the Lok Sabha are elected from among its members by a simple majority of members present and voting in the House. As a result, there are no specific qualifications for being Speaker.

Deputy Speaker

If the Speaker of the Lok Sabha is absent due to death or sickness, the Deputy Speaker of the Lok Sabha serves as the presiding officer. In India, the role of Deputy Speaker is traditionally given to the opposition party.

The Deputy Speaker is elected for a 5-year term from among the members of the Lok Sabha at the first meeting after the general elections. They remain in office until they resign or cease to be a member of the Lok Sabha. They may be suspended from office by a resolution passed by an **effective majority** of members of the Lok Sabha.

After eliminating the vacancies, the majority of an efficient majority should be 50 per cent or more of the total power of the chamber. Since, the Deputy Speaker is responsible for the Lok Sabha, only the successful majority in the Lok Sabha can remove him. There is no need to resign from their original party through as a Deputy Speaker, they have to remain impartial.

Parliamentary Secretary

- The position of Parliamentary Secretary is one of the highest-ranking government positions.
- The Parliamentary Secretaries are appointed by India's Prime Minister.
- Their primary responsibility is to assist cabinet ministers and even the Prime Minister.
- A Parliamentary Secretary is also responsible for a variety of **departmental** and **parliamentary functions**.
- They work closely with cabinet Ministers and are also responsible for department-related public and House Duties.
- The Parliamentary Secretary in the House serves as a point of contact for ministers, senators and other members of the House.
- They contribute to the development of relationships within the government committee.
- They also have an important role to play in the company of the cabinet members.
- In the absence of a minister, they will be kept responsible for answering policy questions in the House.

Chapter Practice

Objective Questions

• Multiple Choice Questions

1. Indian Parliament is divided into .... houses.
   (a) One　　　　　　　(b) Two
   (c) Three　　　　　　(d) None of these

Ans. (b) Indian Parliament is divided into two Houses i.e. House of the People (Lok Sabha) and Council of States (Rajya Sabha).

2. Rajya Sabha members are ....
   (a) Nominated by the member of Lok Sabha.
   (b) Directly Elected by the member of Lok Sabha.
   (c) Indirectly elected by the elected members of the State Legislative Assembly.
   (d) Indirectly elected by the elected members of the State Legislative Council.

Ans. (c) Its members are indirectly elected by the elected members of the State Legislative Assembly.

3. The number of members to be elected from each State has been fixed by the .... Schedule of the Constitution.
   (a) Second　　　　　　(b) Ninth
   (c) Fifth　　　　　　　(d) Fourth

Ans. (d) The number of members to be elected from each State has been fixed by the Fourth Schedule of the Constitution.

4. Consider the following statements.
   1. Every two years, one-fourth members of the Rajya Sabha complete their term and elections are held for one-fourth seats only.
   2. The Rajya Sabha is never dissolved and is called the permanent House of the Parliament.
   Which of the statements given above is / are correct?
   (a) Only 1　　　　　　(b) Only 2
   (c) Both 1 and 2　　　(d) None of these

Ans. (b) Every two years, one-third members of the Rajya Sabha complete their term and elections are held for one-third seats only. Hence, statement (1) is incorrect.

Thus, the Rajya Sabha is never dissolved and is called the permanent House of the Parliament. Hence, statement 2 is correct. Therefore (b) is the correct statement.

5. Nominated members of Rajya Sabha are appointed by
   (a) Chairman of the Rajya Sabha
   (b) President
   (c) Speaker of the Rajya Sabha
   (d) Chief Justice of India

Ans. (b) Apart from elected members, Rajya Sabha also has twelve nominated members nominated by the President and these nominations are made from among persons who are in the fields of literature, science, art and social service.

6. Parliament refers to .... legislature, whereas, the legislature in a state is known as .... legislature.
   (a) National, Legislative Assembly
   (b) National, Legislative Council
   (c) National, State
   (d) Federal Assembly, State

Ans. (c) The National Legislature is referred to as 'Parliament'. State legislature is the name given to the legislature of each state.

7. The .... and .... are directly elected by the people on the basis of Universal Adult Suffrage.
   (a) Lok Sabha, Rajya Sabha
   (b) Legislative Council, State Legislative Assemblies
   (c) Rajya Sabha, State Legislative Assemblies
   (d) Lok Sabha, State Legislative Assemblies

Ans. (d) The Lok Sabha and the State Legislative Assemblies are directly elected by the people on the basis of Universal Adult Suffrage, where the value of vote of every individual is equal.

8. What is the total strength of the House of People?
   (a) 543　　　(b) 554　　　(c) 535　　　(d) 550

Ans. (a) The strength of the Lok Sabha is 543 in addition with two seats to be nominated from Anglo-Indian community by the President.
   Note: 104th Constitutional Amendment Act has removed this provision for nominated member Anglo-Indian Community in Lok Sabha and State Legislative Assemblies.

9. The House can be dissolved by the President on which of the following advice?
(a) Leader of the Opposition
(b) Speaker of the House of the People
(c) Chairman of the Rajya Sabha
(d) Council of and Prime Minister

Ans. (d) The House can be dissolved if the Prime Minister advices the President to dissolve the House and hold fresh elections or if no party or coalition can form the government.

10. The Council of States is called .... and the House of People is called ....
(a) Lok Sabha, Rajya Sabha
(b) Rajya Sabha, Lok Sabha
(c) Vidhan Sabha, Vidhan Parishad
(d) Vidhan Parishad, Vidhan Sabha

Ans. (b) The Council of States is called Rajya Sabha and the House of People is called Lok Sabha.

11. Arrange the following procedure to make law in chronological order.
(i) Bill is sent to committee for recommendation.
(ii) Introduction of the bill in the Parliament.
(iii) A bill has to be passed by both the houses for enactment.
(iv) The bill is then voted by the members.

Select the correct code.
(a) (iii), (i), (iv) and (ii)   (b) (ii), (i), (iv) and (iii)
(c) (iv), (i), (ii) and (iii)   (d) (i), (ii), (iii) and (iv)

Ans. (b) Option (b) is the correct order to make law.

12. Who has the final powers in deciding matters of breach of privilege?
(a) Leader of that House
(b) The President
(c) The presiding officer of the legislature
(d) None of the above

Ans. (c) The presiding officer of the legislature has the final powers in deciding matters of breach of privilege.

13. What are the functions of Parliamentary Committee?
(i) Study the issue of consideration in legislation.
(ii) Study the demands for grants made by various ministries.
(iii) Expenditure incurred by various departments.
(iv) Investigating the cases of corruption.

Which of the statements given above is / are correct?
(a) (i) and (ii)
(b) (i), (iii) and (iv)
(c) (ii), (iii) and (iv)
(d) All of the above

Ans. (d) All these statements are the functions of the Parliamentary Committee. Therefore, (d) is the correct option.

14. Choose the wrong statement.
(a) On account of its composition, Legislature is the most representative of all organs of government.
(b) The Parliament can effectively control the executive and ensure a more responsive government.
(c) The Speaker can resign at any time by writing to the President under his or her hand.
(d) Parliamentary Secretary is appointed by Prime Minister.

Ans. (c) The Speaker can resign at any time by writing to the Deputy Speaker under his or her hand.

15. Study the picture given below and answer the question that follows.

What does this picture represents?
(a) Individual discussion on a budget.
(b) Preparation for electoral role.
(c) Joint Session of Parliament
(d) None of the above

Ans. (a) This picture represents individual discussion on a budget.

• Assertion-Reasoning MCQs

Directions (Q. Nos. 16-20) In the questions given below, there are two statements marked as Assertion (A) and Reason (R). Read the statements and choose the correct option.

Codes
(a) Both A and R are true and R is the correct explanation of A.
(b) Both A and R are true, but R is not the correct explanation of A.
(c) A is true, but R is false.
(d) A is false, but R is true.

16. **Assertion** (A) Financial resources to implement the policies and programmes of the government are granted through the budget.

Reason (R) Preparation and presentation of budget for the approval of the legislature is the constitutional obligation of government.

Ans. (b) Both the statements are correct and reason is not the correct explanation of assertion. Assertion is talking about the financial resource for the implementation of the welfare scheme for the betterment of people whereas Reason is about presentation of budget so that it can get approve from the Parliament.

17. Assertion (A) Anti-defection law, means that a legislator who is elected on one party's ticket is restricted from defecting to another party.

Reason (R) Anti-defection law is mention in the Ninth Schedule of the Constitution.

Ans. (d) Ways to control the behaviour of the member by the presiding officer is anti-defection law, which means that a legislator who is elected on one party's ticket is restricted from defecting to another party.

Anti-defection law is mention in the tenth schedule of the Constitution. It was inserted by the 52nd Constitutional Amendment Act. Hence, reason is not correct.

18. Assertion (A) If a confidence motion against the government is passed, the government loses majority.

Reason (R) The Parliament can effectively control the executive and ensures a more responsive government.

Ans. (c) If a no-confidence motion against the government is passed, the government loses majority. Hence, assertion is incorrect.

The Parliament can effectively control the executive and ensures a more responsive government.

19. Assertion (A) No action can be initiated against a member of Parliament for whatever said in the legislature.

Reason (R) The members have parliamentary privileges.

Ans. (a) No action can be initiated against a member of Parliament for whatever said in the legislature because the members have parliamentary privileges. This is known as parliamentary privileges. Hence both A and R are correct and R is the correct explanation of A.

20. Assertion (A) The Rajya Sabha is elected by MLAs rather than the general public. As a result, the Rajya Sabha was not given certain powers under the constitution.

Reason (R) The Rajya Sabha can criticise the government but not overthrow it.

Ans. (a) The Rajya Sabha is elected by MLAs rather than the general public. As a result, the Rajya Sabha was not given certain powers under the Constitution.

Rajya Sabha can criticise but can't overthrow government because they are elected by the MLAs.

The people are the final authority in a democratic government, as defined by our Constitution. According to this argument, representatives who are directly elected by the people should have the right to remove a government and oversee its finances. Hence, both A and R are correct and R is the correct explanation of A.

• Case Based MCQs

1. Read the passage and answer the questions that follow.

The committee system has reduced the burden on the Parliament. Many important bills have been referred to committees. The Parliament has merely approved the work done in the committees with few occasional alterations. Of course, legally speaking, no bill can become law and no budget will be sanctioned unless approved by the Parliament. But the Parliament rarely rejects the suggestions made by the committees. "The nature of the legislature is such that there are restrictions only so far as procedure is concerned. But in substance there is no restriction, no limitation on the sovereignty of the legislature or Parliament...".

(i) Name the instruments of Parliament to control the executive.
(a) No-Confidence Motion (b) Adjournment Motion
(c) Question Hour (d) All of these

Ans. (d) The instruments of Parliament to control the executive are Adjournment motion, Questions Hour, Zero Hour, No-Confidence Motion are some of the instruments of exercising control.

(ii) Which system has reduced the burden on the Parliament?
(a) Judiciary System (b) Committee System
(c) Legislation (d) None of these

Ans. (b) The committee system has reduced the burden on the Parliament. Many important bills have been referred to committees.

(iii) The word procedure in the above passage refers to ....
(a) Working of the Parliament
(b) Execution of Parliament
(c) Legislation
(d) Judiciary

Ans. (a) The word procedure in the above passage refers to the working of the Parliament.

(iv) The .... of the legislature is the final authority in matters of regulating the business of the legislature.
(a) Presiding Officer (b) President
(c) Speaker (d) Both (a) and (c)

Ans. (d) The Speaker/Presiding officer has the final authority in matter relating to the business in the house.

(v) Consider the following statements.

1. A bill can become a law if it is passed by the majority of the Lok Sabha.
2. No budget will be sanctioned unless approved by the Parliament and received President assent.

Which of the statements given above is / are correct?

(a) Only 1
(b) Only 2
(c) Both 1 and 2
(d) None of the above

Ans. (d) A bill can become a law if it is passed by both the Houses of Parliament. No budget will be sanctioned unless approved by the Parliament. Budget does not need final assent from the President.

PART 2
Subjective Questions

• Short Answer Type Questions

1. Why do we need a Parliament?

Ans. Need for Parliament arises due to the following reasons

- It is a legislative organ of the governemnt. It enables citizens of India to participate in decision making and control the government.
- It contributes to the legislative process and, from time to time introduces new legislation.
- It maintains financial control over the government's revenue, i.e. the government cannot spend public funds without Parliament's permission.
- It is in charge of the government's executive branch. This means that in order for the organ to function, it must have a mandate from Parliament.

2. Discuss the main features of the Indian Parliament.

Ans. The main features of Indian Parliament are as follows

- The Parliament of India is a bicameral legislature.
- The Parliament consists of President, Lok Sabha and Rajya Sabha.
- The upper house of the Parliament is the permanent chamber i.e. it does not dissolve.
- Lower house of the Parliament can be dissolved before expiry of its term.
- The membership of both the houses in Parliament is not equal.
- A person cannot have the membership of both the houses.
- Parliament is the supreme law-making body in India.
- Powers of both the houses are not equal.
- Lok Sabha is more powerful than Rajya Sabha but, in few matters Rajya Sabha has special powers.

3. Upper house is permanent chamber in Bicameral Legislature. Explain.

Ans. In the Bicameral Legislature, there exist two houses, one is the lower house and other one is the upper house. The upper house is permanent, this means, it does not dissolve totally. In India, one-third member of the Rajya Sabha retire in every two years and elections are held for only one-third seats.

So, the members enjoy the tenure of six years, and the house is not dissolved and referred to as permanent House. For example, in Canada, the members to the senate are nominated for the whole of life. In Britain, the House of Lords is hereditary which never cease to exist.

4. Mention the special powers of the Rajya Sabha.

Ans. The special powers of the Rajya Sabha are as follows

- It approves constitutional amendments Bill.
- It exercise control over executive by asking questions, introducing motions and resolutions.
- It participates in the elections and removal of the President, Vice-President, removal of judges of Supreme Court and High Court. It can alone initiate the procedure for removal of Vice-President.
- It can give union Parliament powers to make laws on matters included in the State List.
- It makes laws on any subject in the State List.
- It makes law to create All India Services.

5. Is Indian Parliament a sovereign law-making body?

Ans. No, Indian Parliament is not a sovereign law-making body. The limitations on the law-making power of Parliament are as follows

- Indian Parliament cannot legislate on the subjects given in the State List in ordinary circumstances. It can make laws on State List only, if asked by the Rajya Sabha.
- Parliament cannot make laws in violation of the constitution and Fundamental Rights.
- Judiciary enjoys the power to declare a law passed by the Parliament unconstitutional, if it is in contravention to the constitution.
- The Constitution is the fundamental law of the land in our country. It has defined the authority and jurisdiction of all the three organs of the government and the nature of interrelationship between them. Hence, the Parliament has to operate within the limits prescribed by the Constitution.

6. Elucidate the powers of Lok Sabha.

Ans. The powers of Lok Sabha are as follows

- It makes laws on matters including in the Union List and Concurrent List.
- It can introduce and enact Money Bill and Ordinary Bills.
- It approves proposal for taxation and annual financial statement.

- It controls the executive by asking questions, supplementary questions, resolutions, motions and through no-confidence motion.
- It amends the constitution.
- It approves the proclamation of emergency.
- Lok Sabha elects and removes the President, Vice-President and the Judges of Supreme Court and High Court.
- It establishes committees and commissions and consider their reports.

7. Differentiate between the Powers of Lok Sabha and Rajya Sabha.

Ans. The difference between the Powers of Lok Sabha and Rajya Sabha are

Powers of Lok Sabha	Powers of Rajya Sabha
It can introduce and enact money and non-money bills.	It considers and approve non-money bill and suggest amendments to money bills.
It approves proposal for taxation, budgets and annual financial statements.	It approves constitutional amendments bills.
Lok Sabha controls the executive by asking questions or by passing a resolutions and motions.	It exercise control over executive by asking questions, introducing motions and resolution.
It elects and removes the President, Vice-President and the Judges of the Supreme Court and High Court.	It participate in the elections and removal of the President, Vice-President and the Judges of the Supreme Courts and High Courts.
It establishes committee and commissions and consider their reports.	Its purpose is to protect the power of states.
It makes laws on matter included in the Union List and Concurrent List.	It can give power to Parliament to make laws on matters included in the State List.

8. State your arguments in favour of unicameral legislature.

Ans. The arguments in favour of unicameral legislature are as follows

- **Uniformity in Legislature** It is believed by the pro-unicameral supporters that this system helps to maintain uniformity and unity in the legislature. Laws express the opinion of the people and the people cannot have two opinions on the same subject. Thus, there should be only one chamber to represent the public opinion properly.
- **Saving of Time and Money** Unicameral system leads to saving of time and money. The expenditure to be incurred on the payment of salary and allowances of the members of the other house can be utilised for other useful purposes. When a bill has to be passed only in one house, it saves time.

9. What are the judicial functions of Parliament?

Ans. The important judicial functions of Parliament are given below

- The judicial functions of the Parliament include considering the proposals for removal of President, Vice-President and judges of High Courts and Supreme Court.
- It performs quasi-judicial or semi-judicial functions.
- The Parliament is also empowered to extend the jurisdiction of a High Court to any Centrally administered area or to furnish such a jurisdiction from any such area.
- It may even establish a High Court in a centrally administered area.
- It may establish more courts for getting the law made by it enforced properly.
- In the care of breach of privileges by members of the House the Parliament has a power to punish them.
- It is authorised to frame laws to enforce the orders issued by the Supreme Court.

10. How does the Indian Parliament control the executive?

Ans. The Indian Parliament controls the executive through following ways

- It prevents the domination of personality cult and concentration of power into a sinlge source.
- Parliament ensure executive accountability to the legislature.
- The Parliament can invite attention of Council of Ministers towards the serious problems in the nation through an adjournment motion.
- The ministers are responsible to the Parliament for their actions and policies.
- Parliament enjoys the right of no-confidence motion against the government.
- It controls the executive actions through Question Hour.

11. How does deliberation and discussion keep a control over executive?

Ans. The legislature in Parliamentary system ensures executive accountability at various stages, this can be done through the use of a variety of devices, one of them is deliberation and discussion. The members of the legislature get an opportunity to deliberate on the policy direction of the executive in the law-making process.

Apart from deliberating bills, control may also be exercised during general discussions in the house.

Question Hour Which is held every day during the sessions of Parliament, where ministers have to respond to questions raised by members.

Zero Hour where members are free to raise any matter that they think is important. Half an hour discussion on matters of public importance and adjournment motion are some of the instruments of exercising control.

Among the various instruments of exercising control over executive, the question hour is proved to be the most prevalent and effective.

12. What do you understand by vote of no-confidence?

Ans. A vote of no-confidence is a vote in which members of a group are asked to indicate that they do not support the person or groups in power, usually the government. In a parliamentary form of government, the executive is controlled by the legislature. The cabinet can remain in office so long as it enjoys the confidence of the lower house of the Parliament.

If the Lok Sabha passes a vote of no-confidence against the cabinet or Council of Ministers for wrong policies, then the entire cabinet or Council of Ministers is dissolved and has to resign. Further, fresh elections are to be conducted for a new legislature to form. Vote of no-confidence is to be passed by 50 members of the Lok Sabha in order to control the cabinet or Council of Ministers in the parliamentary form of government.

13. When Joint Session of the Parliament is held?

Ans. The Indian constitution provides for a joint sitting of both house of Parliament. Accordingly, a joint session can be called when

- If a bill is passed by one House and transmitted to the another House, and the other House reject the bill or Houses do not agree on the amendment made to the bill, then under Article 108 the President may summon a joint sitting of the two Houses to resolve the deadlock.
- The Speaker presides over a joint sitting. In the absence of Speaker, the Deputy Speaker of the Lok Sabha preside over it and his absence the sitting is presided over the Deputy Chairman of Rajya Sabha. In a joint sitting no new amendments can be made.

14. Why is the parliamentary committees are referred to as Miniature Legislature?

Ans. Parliamentary committee are referred to as a Miniature Legislature because they are appointed for distinct legislative purpose and for day-to-day business of the house by the parliament. The Parliamentary Committees performs functions such as study the issue of consideration in legislation, study the demands for grants made by various ministries, expenditure incurred by various departments, investigating cases of corruption, etc.

Further, the committee system has occupied a position of eminence in our country and has reduced the burden on the Parliament. Thus, it is referred to as Miniature Legislature.

15. What is Anti-Defection law?

Ans. The anti-defection law punishes individual member of parliament or member of legislation assemblies for leaving party for another. This provision was added by the 52th Amendment Act, 1985.

The presiding officer of the House is the authority who takes final decisions on all such cases. If it is proved that a member has 'defected', then such member loses the membership of the House.

Defection occurs when a member fails to appear in the House when asked by the party leadership to do so, votes against the party's instructions or willingly departs the party's membership.

• Long Answer Type Questions

1. Describe in detail about the upper house or Rajya Sabha. Also discuss about its powers.

Ans. The Rajya Sabha represents the states of India. Its members are indirectly elected by the elected members of the State Legislative Assembly. Representation of seats to the second chamber is done according to the size of the population of the states, that means states with large population will have more seats than the states with less population. Members of the Rajya Sabha are elected for a term of six years and can be re-elected.

All members of the Rajya Sabha do not complete their term at the same time. Every two years, one-third members of the Rajya Sabha complete their term and elections are held for one-third seats only. Thus, the Rajya Sabha is never fully dissolved and is called the permanent house of the Parliament.

Power of Rajya Sabha

- It considers and approves non-money bill and suggests amendments to money bills.
- It approves constitutional amendments bills.
- It exercise control over executive by asking questions, introducing motions and resolutions.
- It participates in the elections and removal of the President, Vice-President, Judges of Supreme Court and High Court.
- It can alone initiate the procedure for removal of Vice-President.
- It can give Union Parliament powers to make laws on matters included in the state list.
- The Rajya Sabha is the representation of states and its purpose is to protect the powers of states, thus, the Union Parliament needs the approval of the Rajya Sabha to alter the matter prescribed in the State List. This provision adds to the strength of the Rajya Sabha.

2. Elucidate the functions of the Parliament.

Ans. The powers and functions of the Parliament are as follows

Legislative Function

- The Parliament is the chief law-making body in the country and often merely approves legislations.
- The task of drafting the bill is done by the bureaucracy under the supervision of the minister concerned.
- The substance and timing of the bill are decided by the cabinet and no major bill is introduced in the Parliament without the approval of the cabinet.
- The most vital function of the Parliament is to ensure that the executive does not overstep its authority and remains responsible to the people who have elected them.

Financial Function

- In a democracy, legislature controls the taxation and its use by the government.
- No new tax can be introduced without the approval of Lok Sabha.
- The financial powers of the Parliament involve the grant of resources to the government to implement its programmes.
- The government has to give an account to the legislature about the expenditure and resources.
- In order to ensure that the government does not overspend, the budget and annual financial statements are prepared.

Debating Function

- The Parliament is the highest forum of debate in the country without any limitation on its power of discussion and the members are free to speak on any matter without fear.
- These discussions constitute the heart of democratic decision making.

Constituent Function

- The Parliament has the power to enact changes to the constitution and both the houses are similar in constituent powers.
- All the amendments have to be approved by a special majority of both the houses of Parliament.

Electoral Functions The Parliament also performs some electoral functions, as it elects the President and Vice-President of India.

Judicial Functions

- The judicial function of the Parliament includes considering the proposals for removal of President, Vice-President and judges of High Courts and Supreme Court.
- It performs quasi-judicial or semi-judicial functions.

3. Describe the law-making procedure in the Parliament of India.

Ans. The detailed procedure followed by Parliament is given below

- **First Stage** Introduction of a bill in the parliament constitute the first stage. A bill can either be introduced in the Lok Sabha or Rajya Sabha, except the money bill which can only be introduced in Lok Sabha.
- **Second Stage** The bill is sent to committee for recommendation and then sent back to the house.
  Third Stage The bill is voted upon and if a non-money bill is passed by one house, it is sent to the other House where it goes through the same procedure.
- **Final Stage** A bill has to be passed by both the houses for enactment and if there is disagreement between the house on the proposed bill, then a joint session of the Parliament is held to resolve the deadlock. If it is money bill, the Rajya Sabha has to give its suggestion or it could delay the passage by 14 days and after that it is deemed to have been passed. Any amendments suggested by Rajya Sabha may or may not be accepted by the Lok Sabha. When the bill is passed by both the houses, it is sent to the President for his assent. Finally, the assent of the President results in the enactment of bill into a law.

4. Explain the devices of legislature to ensure execute accountability.

Ans. The legislature in parliamentary system ensures executive accountability in policy making, implementation of law or policy through various devices which are as follows

- **Deliberation and Discussion** The members of the legislature get an opportunity to deliberate on the policy direction of the executive in the law-making process. The legislature exercise control over the executive during general discussion in the house by Question Hour, Zero Hour, half an hour discussion and adjournment motion. The issue of public interest such as price rise, atrocities on weaker sections, ryots, etc. are questioned.
- **Approval and Refusal of Laws** Parliamentary control is also exercised through its power of ratification, as a bill can become a law only after the approval of both the houses of parliament. A government who has majority in the Lok Sabha also needs the approval of the upper house for a bill to become a law.
- **Financial Control** Financial resources to implement the policies and programmes of the government are granted through budget and the approval of the legislature is the constitutional obligation on the government.
- **No-Confidence Motion** The government has to retain the support of the parties in coalition to maintain its majority in the Lok Sabha. If a no-confidence motion against the cabinet of Council of Ministers is passed by 50 members, the cabinet has to resign.

5. How has the system of parliamentary committee affected the overseeing and appraisal of legislation by the Parliament? **[NCERT]**

Ans. The system of parliamentary committee has influenced the overseeing and appraisal of legislation by the Parliament, as most of decisions regarding the technical points of legislation are referred to these committees.

The Parliament rarely rejects any of the suggestions made by the committee. There are over twenty standing committees related to various departments that works on the issue of budget and its expenditure related to their respective departments. These committees also supervise the bills related to their department that comes in the house. The Joint Parliamentary Committees investigate financial irregularities.

Thus, parliamentary committees have reduced the burden on the legislature and saved time, as the Parliament meets only for a limited time during its sessions. However, on most occasions, the Parliament makes only minor alterations to the draft of the bills, while it approves them. This has diluted the Parliament's appraisal of legislation to a large.

• Case Based Questions

1. Read the passage and answer the questions that follow.

The legislature in parliamentary system ensures executive accountability during policy making, implementation of law or policy through various devices which are Deliberation and Discussion The members of the legislature get an opportunity to deliberate on the policy direction of the executive during law making process. Apart from deliberating on bills, control may also be exercised during general discussions in the House. The Question Hour is held every day during the sessions of Parliament, where ministers have to respond to questions raised by members. Zero Hour where members are free to raise any matter that they think is important, Half an Hour discussion on matters of public importance and adjournment motion are some of the instruments of exercising control. Among the various instruments of exercising control over executive, the question hour is proved to be the most prevalent and effective as the issue of public interest such as price rise, availa- bility of food grains, atrocities on weaker sections, ryots, black marketing, etc. are questioned.

(i) What are the instruments of Parliamentary Control?

(ii) What is Question Hour?

(iii) What is Zero hour?

Ans. (i) Adjournment motion, Questions Hour, Zero Hour, No-Confidence Motion are some of the instruments of exercising control.

(ii) The Question Hour is scheduled for the first hour every day during the sessions of Parliament, where ministers have to respond to questions raised by members .

(iii) Zero hour is the time when Member of Parliament can raise issues of urgent public importance.

2. Read the following passage carefully and answer the questions that follow.

Parliamentary Officials Speaker In our parliamentary democracy, the Speaker's Office plays a critical role. The Speaker's Office has been defined as representing the full authority of the House of Commons, while members of Parliament represent individual constituencies. Speakers serve from the date of their election until the first meeting of the Lok Sabha after the dissolution of the one to which they were elected. He or she is eligible for re-election. The Speaker's position is a constitutional one.

The Speaker is bound by the provisions of the constitution as well as the Rules of Procedure and Conduct of Business in Lok Sabha.

While the Speaker ceases to be a member of the House when the Lok Sabha is dissolved, he or she does not vacate his or her office. The Speaker can resign at any time by writing to the Deputy Speaker under his or her hand. Only a resolution of the House passed by a vote of all members of the House at the time will remove the Speaker from office. The Speaker and Deputy Speaker of the Lok Sabha, the lower House of the Indian Parliament are elected from among its members by a simple majority of members present and voting in the House. As a result, there are no specific qualifications for being Speaker.

(i) What is the tenure of the Speaker of the Lok Sabha?

(ii) Which type of majority is required for the election of Deputy Speaker of the Lok Sabha?

(iii) What is the election procedure to appoint Deputy Speaker of the Lok Sabha?

Ans. (i) Speakers serve from the date of their election until the first meeting of the Lok Sabha after the dissolution of the one to which they were elected. He or she is eligible for re-election.

(ii) The Deputy Speaker of the lower house are elected from among its memeber by a simple majority of members present and voting in the House.

(iii) The Deputy Speaker of the Lok Sabha, the lower House of the Indian Parliament are elected from among its membrs by a simple majority of members present and voting in the House.

4. Observe the cartoon given below and answer the questions that follow.

(i) What does this cartoon represents?

(ii) In response to protests, the opposition typically employs which tactic?

(iii) What is it impacts?

Ans. (i) This cartoon represents public asking question from member of parliament.

(ii) The opposition's serious adopted measure to register their discontent against the administration is the walkout.

(iii) The impact of the over use of this weapon has led to the wastage of the sessions of Parliament, delays in passage of important bills to become act, boycotted the debate and discussions in the Parliament, which serve to be instruments of control over executive.

5. Observe the cartoon given below and answer the questions that follow.

(i) What does this cartoon represents?

(ii) How does the Parliament control over executive financially?

(iii) What are the financial powers of the parliament?

Ans. (i) The cartoon represents the sanction of money to different ministries.

(ii) Every government raises resources through taxation and the Parliament controls taxation. If the government wants to introduce new tax, it has to get the approval of the Lok Sabha which is the lower house of Parliament.

(iii) The financial powers of the Parliament are

- Grant of resources to the government, to implement the programmes.
- The government has to give an account of the money spent and resources it wishes to raise to the legislature.
- It ensures that the government does not mis-spend or over-spend. Budget and annual financial statements are presented before the Parliament.

Chapter Test

- **Objective Type Questions**

  1 The members of Rajya Sabha are indirectly elected by the elected members of ....
     - (a) Lok Sabha
     - (b) State Lagislative Assemblies
     - (c) Both Lok Sabha and State Assemblies
     - (d) They are elected directly by the people.

  2 The members of which among the following are elected on the basis of Universal Adult Suffrage?
     - (a) Rajya Sabha
     - (b) Lok Sabha
     - (c) Vidhan Sabha
     - (d) President

  3 A Constitnent Amendment Bill has to be approved by both Houses of Parliament by a .... majority.
     - (a) Simple
     - (b) Absolute
     - (c) Special
     - (d) None of these

  4 Indian Parliament is divided into .... houses.
     - (a) One
     - (b) Two
     - (c) Three
     - (d) None of these

  5 Who has the final powers in deciding matters of breach of privilege?
     - (a) Leader of that House
     - (b) The President
     - (c) The presiding officer of the legislature
     - (d) None of the above

- **Short Answer Type Questions**

  1 Mention the powers of Rajya Sabha.

  2 Write a note on composition of the Parliament.

  3 How does Parliament control the executive?

  4 Rajya Sabha is a permanent chamber. Explain.

  5 Describe the committee system in Indian Parliament.

  6 What is the need and importance of Parliament in a democracy?

  7 How is a Money Bill different from an Ordinary Bill?

- **Long Answer Type Questions**

  1 Describe the limitations on the powers of the Parliament.

  2 Discuss the mutual relations between the two houses of Parliament.

  3 Describe the powers and functions of the Indian Parliament.

  4 State the functions and powers of State Legislature.

Executive

In this Chapter...

- Meaning of Executive
- Parliamentary Executive in India
- Council of Minister
- Coalition Government
- Permanent Executive : Bureaucracy

Legislature, executive and judiciary are the three main organs of the government and together they perform the functions of the government, maintain law and order and work for the welfare of the people. In a parliamentary form of government, executive and the legislature are interdependent, the legislature controls the executive and vice-versa. The Constitution mandates that they collaborate and maintain a balance among themselves.

Meaning of Executive

A body of persons that looks after the implementation of rules and the regulations of organisation in actual practice is known as the **Executive**. The executive take policy decisions or big decisions and supervise and coordinate the routine administrative functioning. Every formal organisation has a group of people who serve as the organisation's chief administrators or executives of that organisation. Some office holders make decisions about policies, rules and regulations and others carry out those decisions in the organisation's day-to-day operations.

Functions of the Executive

Executive is the branch of the government which holds the responsibility of **implementation of laws and policies** adopted by the legislature. The functions of the executive are

- Executive is involved in framing the policies of the government.
- The official designations of executive vary from country to country, according to the form of government one has adopted.
- The executive branch includes the President, Prime Minister and Ministers and also extends to the administer machinery, like the Civil Servants.

- The head of the government and their ministers charged with the overall responsibility of the government policy are together known as **Political Executive**.
- The body responsible for the day to day administration are called the **Permanent Executive**.

Different Types of Executives

Types of executives in Parliamentary System, Presidential System and Semi-Presidential System are discussed below

Parliamentary System

The system in which the formulation of policies and enactment of the laws of a country are done by the Parliament, are called Parliamentary system. In this system, the Prime Minister is the **Head of the government** while the President or Monarch is the **nominal head** of the state.

The role of President or Monarch is primarily ceremonial and the Prime Minister with the cabinet exercises effective power. For example Germany, Italy, Japan, UK, Portugal, India, Canada are some of the countries which follow the Parliamentary system. In the case of Japan, the Emperor is the head of the state and the Prime Minister is head of the government.

Presidential System

In this system, President is the head of the state as well as the head of the government. For example USA, Brazil and most nations of Latin America has adopted the Presidential system. In this system, the President is directly elected by the people and he is not responsible to the legislature.

Semi-Presidential System

A Semi-Presidential system is the form of Government which has both the President and the Prime Minister, where the President is the head of the state and the Prime Minister is the head of the government.

Prime Minister and the Council of Ministers are responsible to the legislature. But, unlike the Parliamentary system, the President may possess significant day-to-day powers.

In this system, it is possible that the President and the Prime Minister, sometimes they may belong to the same party and at times they may belong to two different parties and thus, would confront each other. For example, France, Russia, Sri Lanka, etc. are the countries which follow the Semi-Presidential system.

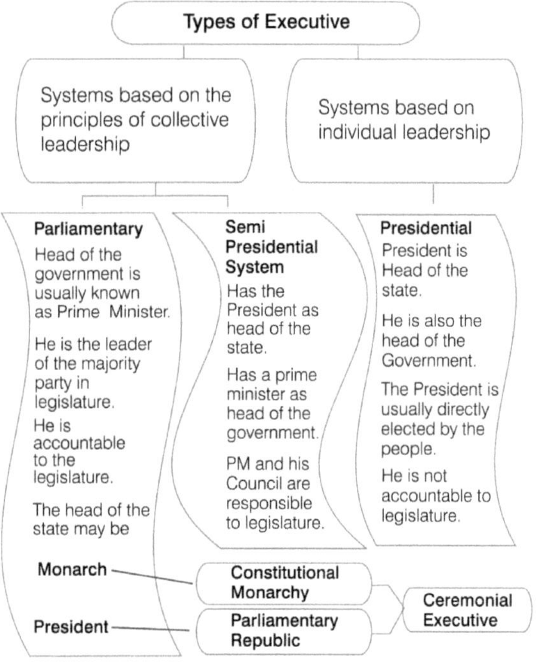

Types of Executive

Semi-Presidential System in Sri Lanka

The Constitution of Sri Lanka was amended to introduce the system of Executive Presidency in 1978. Under this system people directly elect the President. It may happen that both the President and the Prime Minister belong to the same political party or to different political parties.

Under the Constitution the President has more power, he choose the Prime Minister from the party who has the majority in Parliament. He is not only the elected Head of State or the Commander-in-Chief but also the Head of the Government.

The term of office of the President is six years. He can be removed except by a resolution in the Parliament passed by at least two-thirds of the total number of Members of Parliament.

If it is passed by not less than one half of the total number of members and speaker is satisfied that such allegations merit inquiry then the Speaker can report the matter to the Supreme Court.

Parliamentary Executive in India

India follows the Parliamentary system of executive. In the Parliamentary system, the executives are controlled by the representatives of people. Under the Acts of 1919 and 1935 India already had some experience of running the Parliamentary system.

India had the alternative of presidential form of government which puts much emphasis on the President as the **Chief Executive** and source of all executive power. The makers of the Indian Constitution in order to provide enough safeguards to check against the personality cult, adopted the parliamentary form of government both at the centre and state level.

In this system, there are mechanisms that ensure that the executive will be answerable to and controlled by the legislature or people's representatives. According to the parliamentary form of government, Executive at the National Level comprise of the **President** (a formal Head of the State) and the **Prime Minister** with his **Council of Ministers** whereas, Executive at the State Level Compriser the **Governor** and the **Chief Minister** with his Council of Ministers to run the government.

President

The President is the nominal head of the state and the constitution of India vests the executive powers of the union formally in the President. The President exercises these powers through the Council of Ministers headed by the Prime Minister.

The President is elected indirectly for a period of five years. The President is elected by the elected **MLAs** and **MPs**, according to the Principle of Proportional Representation with single transferable vote.

The President can be removed from office only by the Parliament by following the **impeachment**[1] procedure which requires the special majority of both the Houses of Parliament. The only ground for impeachment is the violation of the constitution.

Power and Functions of President

Article 74 (1) of the Indian Constitution stipulates that there shall be a Council of Minister headed by the Prime Minister to aid and advise the President who shall exercise his functions in accordance with such advice. The President has wide range of **Executive**, **Legislative**, **Judicial** and **Emergency powers** which can be exercised only on the advice of Council of Ministers headed by the Prime Minister.

---

1. **Impeachment** A removal process charged against a government funtionary.

The Prime Minister and the Council of Ministers have support of the majority in the Lok Sabha and they are the real executive. In most of the cases the President has to follow the advice of the Council of Ministers.

Discretionary Powers of President

Constitutionally, the President has the right to be informed of all matters and deliberations (discussions) of the Council of Ministers. The Prime Minister is obliged (required) to furnish all the information that the President may call for.

Besides this, there are three situations where President exercises his discretionary powers

(i) When the President thinks that the advice rendered to him has certain flaws or legal breakdown or it is not in the interests of the country, the President can ask the Council of Ministers to reconsider the decision.

However, if the Council of Ministers send back the same advice, then the President would be bound to consider that advice or decision.

(ii) The President also has a **veto power** by which he can withhold or refuse to give assent to Bills passed by the Parliament other than Money Bill. Every bill passed by the Parliament goes to the President for his assent to become a law.

The President can send the bill back to the Parliament for reconsideration, and if the Parliament passes the same bill again and sends it back to the President, then the president is bound to give assent to the bill, as the veto power is limited.

The President can just keep the bill pending with him without any time limit and enjoys informal power to use this veto in effective manner which is referred to as Pocket Veto.

(iii) In a situation after the election where no leader has acquired majority in the Lok Sabha to form government, then the President exercises his discretion in judging who may have the support of the majority or who can actually form and run the government.

However, this discretion comes out of political circumstances. In ordinary circumstances, if the Council of Ministers are removed as they depend on the support of the majority in legislature, then the President has the power to make a choice in appointing the Prime Minister to run the government of the country.

Vice-President

The Vice-President is elected for five-years. The only difference between his election and that of the President is that representatives of State Legislatures are not included in the electoral college. The Vice-President may be removed from his office by a resolution of the Rajya Sabha passed by a majority and agreed to it by the Lok Sabha.

When the President's office becomes vacant due to death, resignation, expulsion by impeachment, or other factors, the (removal). The Vice-President acts as the President only until a new President is elected. **BD Jatti** acted as President on the death of **Fakhruddin Ali Ahmed** until a new President was elected. Vice-President serves as the ex-officio Chairman of the Rajya Sabha.

Prime Minister

As the head of the Council of Ministers, the Prime Minister becomes the most important functionary of the government in our country. In a Parliamentary system, it is essential for the Prime Minister to enjoy the support of the majority in the Lok Sabha.

However, the Prime Minister loses his office if the majority is lost. Formally, a leader who has the support of majority is appointed by the President as Prime Minister and then the Prime Minister decides the Council of Ministers.

The Prime Minister and all the Ministers have to be members of the Parliament and in case someone becomes the Prime Minister or minister without being an MP, such person needs to get elected to the Parliament within a period of six months.

> ### President's Role in Choosing the Prime Minister
> After 1977, India's party politics grew more competitive and there have been numerous instances in which no single political party has held a clear majority in the Lok Sabha. In such circumstances, what does the President do? In the March 1998 elections, no political party or coalition received a majority. The BJP and its partners won 251 seats, falling short of a majority by 21 votes. President KR Narayanan followed a rigorous method.

Powers and Functions of Prime Minister

In India, the Prime Minister enjoys a pre-eminent place in the government by following ways:

- The allocation of ranks and portfolios to the ministers is done by the Prime Minister depending upon the seniority and political importance. The ranks of Cabinet Minister or Minister of State or Deputy Minister are assigned by the Prime Minister and the same is done by the Chief Minister in the state level government.

- The Council of Ministers comes into existence only after the Prime Minister has taken oath of office, hence the Council of Ministers cannot exist without the Prime Minister.

- The death or resignation of the Prime Minister automatically dissolves the Council of Ministers but the death, dismissal, resignation of minister only creates a ministerial vacancy.

- The Prime Minister acts as a link between the Council of Ministers on one hand and the President and Parliament together on the other hand.

- It is constitutionally mandatory for the Prime Minister to communicate to the President all decisions of the Council of Ministers relating to the administrative affair of the Union and proposals of legislation. The Prime Minister is involved in all crucial decisions of the government and decides on the policies of the government.

Thus, the power exercised by the Prime Minister flows from various sources, such as, control over the Council of Ministers, leadership of Lok Sabha, command over bureaucratic machinery, etc.

Council of Ministers

The Council of Ministers are also appointed by the **President** on the advice of the **Prime Minister** and is collectively responsible to the Lok Sabha, which means that a Minister who loses confidence of the Lok Sabha is obliged to resign. Collective responsibility implies that a vote of no confidence even against a single minister leads to the resignation of the entire Council of Ministers and further, it also indicates that if a minister does not agree with a policy or decision, the minister either accept the decision or resign.

Size of Council of Ministers

91st Amendment Act, 2003 stated that the size of the Council of Ministers shall not exceed 15 per cent of total number of members of the Lok Sabha or the state legislative assembly, as the case may be.

State Executive

At the state level, a similar parliamentary executive exists with some variations. The variations are that the Governor is appointed by the President on the advice of the Central government and has more discretionary powers and the Chief Minister is the leader of the majority party in the assembly appointed by the Governor.

Coalition Government

Coalition government is a group of advisors created when various political parties or regional parties join forces to manage and regulate the country. If none of the parties wins an absolute majority in the general election, the government is formed by a coalition of more than two parties.

Since 1989, the system of Coalition Government was introduced in India and many of such governments could not remain in power for the full term of Lok Sabha. These developments have affected the working of the parliamentary executive in following ways

- It resulted in growing discretionary role of the President in selection of the Prime Minister.

- The coalition nature of Indian politics, has necessitated much more consultation between political partners, leading to erosion of prime ministerial authority.
- It has also brought restrictions on the privileges of the Prime Minister, like choosing the ministers and deciding their ranks and portfolios.
- The policies and programmes of the government cannot be decided by the Prime Minister alone, as the political parties of different ideologies come together to form government.
- It has led to a lot of negotiations and compromises in policy formulation.

In the state the Chief Minister is the leader of Majority party in Assembly, like the Prime Minister.

Permanent Executive : Bureaucracy

Bureaucracy[2] or administrative machinery is one of the executive organ of the government who works as a permanent employee and are assigned the task of assisting the ministers in formulating policies and implementing these policies. The bureaucracy is politically neutral which means that the bureaucracy will not take any political position on policy matters.

In a democracy, the elected representatives and the ministers are in charge of the government and the administration is under their control and supervision. In the Parliamentary system, the legislature also exercises control over the administration. The administrative officers cannot act in violation of the policies adopted by the legislature and the machinery is also made politically accountable.

Indian Bureaucracy

The Indian bureaucracy is an enormously complex system consisting of the **All India Services**, **State Services**, **employees of the local governments**, **technical** and **managerial staff**.

India has developed a professional administrative infrastructure. Simultaneously, this apparatus is rendered politically accountable. Political neutrality is also expected of the bureaucracy. This implies that the bureaucracy will refrain from taking a political stance on policy issues.

In a democracy, it is always possible for a party to lose elections for the new government to seek to implement new policies in place of the former administration's programmes. In such a case, it is the administrative machinery's job to engage sincerely and efficiently in the policy's development and implementation.

---

2. **Bureaucracy** Civil services or administration that forms the permanent executive.

It is the duty of the administrative machinery to faithfully and efficiently participate in drafting policy and its implementation. In order to make the bureaucracy more representative, the constitution also ensures that all the sections of the society including the weaker sections have the opportunity to be a part of the bureaucracy.

For this purpose, the constitution has provided for reservation of jobs for *Dalits* and *Adivasis* and reservation for women and backward classes. So that social inequalities will not come in the way of recruitment to the civil service.

The UPSC selects people for the **Indian Administrative Service** (IAS) and the **Indian Police Service** (IPS), which form the backbone of the state's higher bureaucracy. The Collector of a district is the most powerful government official in the district. An IAS or IPS official is allocated to a specific state and works under the direction of the state government.

The IAS or IPS officers, on the other hand, are appointed by the Central Government, can return to the service of the Central Government and most crucially, can only be disciplined by the Central Government.

This means that the Central Government supervises and controls the principal administrative officers of the states. Apart from the IAS and IPS officers recruited by the UPSC, officers appointed by the State Public Service Commissions are in charge of the state's government.

The members of civil services of bureaucracy is impartially selected on the basis of merit by the Union Public Service Commission (UPSC) at the centre, and the similar Public Service Commission is provided for the states also. For recruitment into services of state, the members of the commission are appointed for a fixed term and their removal or suspension is subject to a thorough enquiry made by a judge of the Supreme Court.

Therefore, bureaucracy is an instrument through which welfare policies of the government must reach the people.

Classification of Civil Services

Chapter Practice

Objective Questions

• Multiple Choice Questions

1. Which one of the following is not the organ of the government?
   (a) Constitution   (b) Executive
   (c) Legislature   (d) Judiciary

Ans. (a) Legislature, executive and judiciary are the three organ of the government.

2. Who is responsible to control the executive?
   (a) President   (b) Legislature
   (c) Judiciary   (d) Both (a) and (c)

Ans. (b) Legislature controls the executive.

3. The body responsible for the day-to-day administration is called ....
   (a) Political Executive
   (b) Permanent Executive
   (c) Legislature
   (d) Judiciary

Ans. (b) The body responsible for the day to day administration is called Permanent Executive.

4. Which type of executive system does Russia follow?
   (a) Presidential   (b) Parliamentary
   (c) Semi-Presidential   (d) Semi-Parliamentary

Ans. (c) Russia has a Semi-Presidential system in which the President is the head of state and the Prime Minister is the head of government, both of which are appointed by the President.

5. In Presidential System, the President is .... elected by the ....
   (a) directly, people
   (b) indirectly, legislature
   (c) indirectly, people
   (d) directly, legislature

Ans. (a) In Presidential System, the President is directly elected by the people. Indian Parliament is divided into two Houses i.e., House of the People (Lok Sabha) and Council of States (Rajya Sabha).

6. A Semi-Presidential system is the form of Government, the .... is the head of the state and the .... is the head of the government.
   (a) President, Prime Minister
   (b) Prime Minister, President
   (c) Prime Minister, Monarch
   (d) Monarch, Prime Minister

Ans. (a) A Semi-Presidential system is the form of government which has both the President and Prime Minister, where the President is the head of the state and the Prime Minister is the head of the government.

7. In which of the following system of government there are mechanisms that ensure that the executive will be answerable to and controlled by the legislature or people's representatives?
   (a) Semi-Presidential system   (b) Presidential system
   (c) One Party system   (d) Parliamentary system

Ans. (d) In the Parliamentary system of government there are mechanisms that ensure that the executive will be answerable to and controlled by the legislature or people's representatives.

8. The Constitution of India vests the executive power of the union formally in the ....
   (a) Prime Minister   (b) Chief Minister
   (c) President   (d) Vice-President

Ans. (c) The President is the nominal head of the state and the Constitution of India vests the executive powers of the union formally in the President.

9. Who is the part of electoral college to election of the President?
   (i) Elected member of the both the House of Parliament.
   (ii) Nominated member of the both the House of Parliament.
   (iii) Elected member of the State Legislative Assembly
   (iv) Elected member of Legislative Council.

   Select the correct options.
   (a) (i) and (ii)   (b) (i), (ii) and (iii)
   (c) (i) and (iii)   (d) All of these

Ans. (c) The President is elected by the members of the both the House of Parliament and elected member of the State Legislative Assemblies.

10. Which type of veto power used by the President in the statement given below?

The President can just keep the bill pending with him without any time limit.

(a) Qualified Veto   (b) Suspensive Veto
(c) Pocket Veto   (d) Absolute Veto

Ans. (c) The President can just keep the bill pending with him without any time limit and enjoys informal power to use this veto in effective manner which is referred to as Pocket Veto.

11. Who is the ex-officio Chairman of the Rajya Sabha?

(a) Speaker of the House of People.
(b) Person appointed by the member of Rajya Sabha.
(c) Person nominated by the President.
(d) Vice-President.

Ans. (d) Vice-President serves as the ex-officio Chairman of the Rajya Sabha.

12. If no political party or coalition received a majority in the general election then how does the President appoint the Prime Minister?

(a) By consultation with his secretary
(b) By consultation with the last ruling party
(c) By his own discretion
(d) None of the above

Ans. (c) In this situation the President use his discretionary power. In the March 1998 elections, no political party or coalition received a majority.

13. Who allocates ranks and portfolios to the ministers?

(a) Prime Minister   (b) President
(c) Vice-President   (d) None of these

Ans. (a) The allocation of ranks and portfolios to the ministers is done by the Prime Minister depending upon the seniority and political importance.

14. What is the total strength of the Council of Minister?

(a) 10%   (b) 20%
(c) 15%   (d) There is no limit

Ans. (c) 91st Amendment stated that the size of the Council of Ministers shall not exceed 15 per cent of total number of members of the Lok Sabha or the State Legislative Assembly, as the case may be.

Note In the case of Delhi, it is 10%.

15. The policies and programmes of the government cannot be decided by the .... alone.

(a) Home Minister
(b) Prime Minister
(c) President
(d) Leader of the Political Party

Ans. (b) The policies and programmes of the government cannot be decided by the Prime Minister alone, as the political parties of different ideologies come together to form government.

16. Consider the following statements related to Indian bureaucracy.

(i) The Indian bureaucracy consisting of the All India Services, State Services, employees of the local governments technical and managerial staff.

(ii) There is no provision in the constitution which ensures that all the sections of the society including the weaker sections have the opportunity to be a part of the bureaucracy.

Select the incorrect statements.

(a) Only (i)   (b) Only (ii)
(c) Both (i) and (ii)   (d) None of these

Ans. (b)

- All the government servants are the part of bureaucracy. Hence statement (i) is correct.
- In order to make the bureaucracy more representative, the constitution has provided for reservation of jobs for Dalits and Adivasis and reservation for women and backward classes. Hence statement (ii) is incorrect. Therefore, (b) is the correct option.

• Assertion-Reasoning MCQs

Directions (Q. Nos. 17-20) In the questions given below, there are two statements marked as Assertion (A) and Reason (R). Read the statements and choose the correct option.

Codes
(a) Both A and R are true and R is the correct explanation of A.
(b) Both A and R are true, but R is not the correct explanation of A.
(c) A is true, but R is false.
(d) A is false, but R is true.

17. Assertion (A) A body of persons that looks after the implementation of rules and regulations of an organisation is known as the executive.

Reason (R) The executive branch includes the President, Prime Minister and Ministers and also extends to the administer machinery, like the Civil Servants.

Ans. (a) Both the statements are true, but R is the correct explanation of A. Executive is responsible for the implementation of policies and that can be done by the Prime Minister, President, Civil Servants which are the parts of Executive.

18. Assertion (A) Under the Acts of 1919 and 1935 India already had some experience of running the Parliamentary system.

Reason (R) India follows the Parliamentary system of executive.

Ans. (b) Both the statements are true, but R is not the correct explanation of A. India follows the Parliamentary system of executive because Under the Acts of 1919 and 1935 India already had some experience of running the Parliamentary system.

19. Assertion (A) The constitution vests the executive powers of the union in the President of India.

Reason (R) The President of India is the constitution head of the state.

Ans. (a) Both A and R are true and R is the correct explanation of A because the President is the nominal head of the state and the Constitution of India vests the executive powers of the union formally in the President. The President exercises these powers through the Council of Ministers headed by the Prime Minister.

20. Assertion (A) If the Parliament passes the same bill again after reconsideration and sends it back to the President, then the President is not bound to give assent to the bill.

Reason (R) The President also has a veto power by which he can withhold or refuse to give assent to Bills passed by the Parliament.

Ans. (d) Assertion is false and Reason is the true statement. The President has a veto power by which he can withhold or refuse to give assent to bills passed by the Parliament or he can pass the bill to the Parliament for reconsideration and if the Parliament passes the same bill again and sends it back to the President, then the President is bound to give assent to the bill.

• Case Based MCQs

1. Read the passage and answer the questions the follow.

President is the formal head of the government. In this formal sense, the President has wide ranging Executive, Legislative, Judicial and Emergency powers. In a Parliamentary System, these powers are in reality used by the President only on the advice of the Council of Ministers.

The Prime Minister and the Council of Ministers have support of the majority in the Lok Sabha and they are the real executive. In most of the cases, the President has to follow the advice of the Council of Ministers. "We did not give him any real power but we have made his position one of authority and dignity. The constitution wants to create neither a real executive nor a mere figurehead, but a head that neither reigns nor governs; it wants to create a great figurehead..."

(i) Which organ of the executive is mentioned in the passage?
(a) Authority of the President
(b) Legitimacy of Prime Minister
(c) Both (a) and (b)
(d) Neither (a) nor (b)

Ans. (a) Authority of the President is mentioned in the passage.

(ii) .... is the nominal head of the government.
(a) Vice-President   (b) President
(c) Chief Minister   (d) Council of Minister

Ans. (b) President is the nominal head of the government. In this formal sense, the President has wide ranging Executive, Legislative, Judicial and Emergency powers.

(iii) Name the powers of the President.
(a) Executive   (b) Legislative
(c) Emergency   (d) All of these

Ans. (d) President is the formal head of the government. In this formal sense, the President has wide ranging Executive, Legislative, Judicial and Emergency powers.

(iv) President follows the advice of ....
(a) Council of Ministers   (b) Parliamentary Secretaries
(c) Chief Minister   (d) Prime Minister

Ans. (a) In most of the cases, the President has to follow the advice of the Council of Ministers.

(v) Consider the following statements.
1. Constitution makers did not give any real power to the Prime Minister but they have made his position one of authority and dignity.
2. The real executive is Council of Minister headed by the Prime Minister.

Which of the statements given above is / are correct?
(a) Only 1   (b) Only 2
(c) Both (1) and (2)   (d) None of these

Ans. (b) Constitution makers did not give any real power to the President but they have made his position one of authority and dignity. Hence, statement 1 is incorrect.

The real executive is Council of Minister headed by the Prime Minister. Hence, statement 2 is correct. Therefore, (b) is the correct option.

PART 2
Subjective Questions

• Short Answer Type Questions

1. Write down the merits of a good executive.

Ans. The organ of the government that primarily looks after the function of implementation and administration is called the executive.

The merits of a good executive are

• It looks after the administration of law and order in the country, so that the law breakers do not find an opportunity to carry out their evil intentions.

• It should avoid financial fluctuations in the country to maintain stability in economy.

• A good executive sees that the national boundaries are preserved and there is no danger from external aggression.

• It should have the capacity to accommodate all the sections of the society in policy and law.

2. What are the functions of the executive?

Ans. The functions of the executive are

- It is involved in framing the policies of the government.
- The primary function of the executive is to enforce laws and to maintain law and order in the state.
- All the major appointments are made by the Chief Executive. For example, the President of India appoints the Chief Justice and other judges of the Supreme Court and High Courts, Ambassadors, Advocate General of India, etc.
- The members of the civil service are appointed by the Chief Executive.
- It is the responsibility of executive to decide as to which treaties are to be signed with which other countries.
- There are two division of executive; one is the political executive charged with the overall responsibility of the government policy and the other is the permanent executive that look after the day-to-day administration.

3. The Parliamentary System of executive vests many powers in the legislature for controlling the executive. Why do you think is it necessary to control the executive?   **[NCERT]**

Ans In a Parliamentary System, the Prime Minister is head of the government along with the President as nominal Head of the government. The executive is responsible to the Parliament and holds power till it enjoys the confidence of the Parliament.

It is necessary for the legislature to control the executive because

- To ensure accountability of the executive.
- The various mechanisms ensures that the executive is answerable and controlled by the people's representatives so that there is transparency and accountability.
- The control on the executive is must so that it works according to the laws and checks deviation of any kind.
- It also prevents the domination of personality cult and provides a check on arbitrary functioning and concentration of power into a single source.

4. What is the Presidential and Semi-Presidential system of government?

Ans. **Presidential system** is the form of government where the President is the head of the state as well as the head of the government and the office of the President is very powerful in both theory and practice.

In this system, the President is directly elected by the people and he is not accountable to the legislature. For example, USA, Brazil and most nations of Latin America opted the Presidential system of government.

A Semi-Presidential system is the form of Government which has both the President and the Prime Minister, where the President is the head of the state and the Prime Minister is the head of the government.

5. How can the President of India be removed?

Ans. The President of India can be removed from his office before the expiry of his term by the process of impeachment. He can be impeached only for 'violation of constitution'. The power of impeachment of the President is vested in the Parliament. The impeachment procedure can be initiated in either House of the Parliament. The charge must come in the form of proposal contained in a resolution which must be signed by at least one-fourth of the total membership of the House.

Such a resolution must be passed by 2/3 majority of the total membership of the House, then it is sent to the other House. And if the other House also passes it with the 2/3 majority, only then the President can be removed.

6. The President is an essential part of Parliament in India. Do you agree with this statement?

Ans. Yes, the President is an essential part of Parliament. According to the Indian Constitution, all the legislative powers of the centre is given to the Parliament. The Parliament consist of President, Lok Sabha and Rajya Sabha. Similar to the British emperor, the President is an integral part of the Parliament. The President can call both the houses for session. He can dissolve the Lok Sabha.

Any bill passed by the Parliament cannot become an act unless it is signed by the President. He has the authority to address both the houses jointly or separately. He can issue ordinance if both the houses are not in session and the circumstances are compelling for the law.

7. Can the President become a dictator during emergency?

Ans. The President cannot become a dictator during emergency due to the following reasons

- He can declare emergency only when the Council of Ministers sends such a recommendation to him in writing.
- The proclamation of emergency made by the President must be approved by the Parliament within one month. If the Parliament does not give its approval, it will cease to operate at the expiry of one month from the date of its declaration.
- If after getting approval by the Parliament, President tries to become dictator, he can be removed by the Parliament by the method of impeachment.

8. Write a short note on Vice-President?

Ans. The Vice-President serves as the ex-officio Chairman of the Rajya Sabha. The Vice-President is elected by both the Member of Parliament (elected and nominated) for five year term. The member of state legislature does not participate in the election process of Vice-President as it is in the case of President.

The Vice-President may be removed from his office by a resolution of the Rajya Sabha passed by a majority and agreed to it by the Lok Sabha.

When the President's office becomes vacant due to death, resignation, expulsion by impeachment or other factors, the (removal). The Vice-President acts as the President only until a new President is elected. BD Jatti acted as President on the death of Fakhruddin Ali Ahmed until a new President was elected.

9. What do you understand by the dominance of executive leadership?

Ans. In the Parliamentary system, the legislature is formed mainly by the elected representatives because the leader of political party who gets the majority is called upon by the President to form the Government.

The Parliament enjoys many powers, even to pass no-confidence motion against the Prime Minister and his Council of Ministers to remove them from office. But in fact, the Prime Minister leads the Parliament. Whenever, he wants he can dissolve the Lok Sabha. Hence, it is considered as dominance of executive leadership.

10. Write a short note on individual responsibility of ministers.

Ans. Along with collective responsibility, a minister is individually responsible for handling the charge of his department efficiently and in accordance with the accepted policies. He is responsible for the cases in the department incurred due to mishandling and due to mismanagement. The minister is morally bound for it.

Similarly, if a minister is involved in corrupt practices or misuse of public money or some criminal case or murder, etc. he is individually responsible for it.

11. Discuss the powers and functions of the Prime Minister.

Ans. As the head of the Council of Ministers, the Prime Minister becomes the most important functionary of the government in our country. It is essential for the Prime Minister to enjoy the support of the majority in the Lok Sabha. The powers and functions of the Prime Minister are

- The council comes into existence only after the Prime Minister has taken oath of office, hence the Council of Ministers cannot exist without the Prime Minister.
- The death, resignation of the Prime Minister automatically dissolves the Council of Ministers.
- The Prime Minister acts as a link between the Council of Ministers and the President on one hand and the Parliament and President on the other hand.
- It is mandatory, constitutionally for the Prime Minister to communicate to the President all decisions regarding the administrative affairs of the union and purpose of legislation.

12. Why is the Prime Minister considered very powerful? Explain.

Ans. The Prime Minister is considered a very powerful person because of following reasons

- He has wide ranging powers as head of the government.
- He chairs Cabinet meetings, coordinates the work of different departments.
- He keeps an eye on all departments and he guides, instructs, encourages, advises and warns his ministerial colleagues.
- The agenda of the Cabinet meetings will be prepared by the Cabinet Secretariat in consultation with Prime Minister's office.
- He distributes and redistributes work to the ministers.
- He has the power to dismiss them, when he quits the entire ministry quits. The Prime Minister controls the Cabinet and the parliament through the party.

13. Discuss the relationship between the President and the Prime Minister.

Ans. The relationship between the President and the Prime Minister can be understood with following

- According to the Constitution, the President calls upon the leader of the majority party to form government and appoints the Prime Minister.
- President is the nominal head of state while the Prime Minister is the real head of the state.
- The Prime Minister serves as a link between the President and the Council of Ministers.
- The President is indirectly elected, while the Prime Minister is directly elected and leads the nation. Prime Minister is appointed by the President.

14. Why do you think is the advice of the Council of Ministers binding on the President?　　**[NCERT]**

Ans. The advice of the Council of Ministers is binding on the President in a parliamentary executive because

- The Council of Ministers is an elected executive that has the support of the majority in the legislature.
- It also emphasises the supreme authority of elected representatives in a Republic.
- This arrangement distinctively projects the President as a ceremonial head and limits the powers vested in him/her to avoid conflict within the executive.

Thus, the Executive, Legislative, Judicial and Emergency powers of the President are exercised only on the advice of the Council of Ministers.

15. What are the outcomes of coalition government? Briefly Explain.

Ans. The outcomes of coalition government are as follows

- It resulted in the growing discretionary role of the President in selection of the Prime Minister.
- In the Indian politics, it has necessitated much more consultation between political partners, leading to erosion of prime ministerial authority.

- It has also brought restrictions on the privileges of the Prime Minister like, choosing the ministers and deciding their ranks and portfolios.
- The policies and programmes of the government cannot be decided by the Prime Minister alone, as the political parties of different ideologies come together to form government.
- It has led to a lot of negotiation and compromise in policy formulation.

16. What is the Permanent Executive?

Ans. Bureaucracy or administrative machinery is the permanent Executive. It is one of the executive organs of the government who works as a permanent employee and are assigned the task of assisting the ministries in formulating policies and implementing these policies. The bureaucracy is politically neutral which means that the bureaucracy will not take any political position on policy matters.

In a democracy, the elected representatives and the ministers are in charge of the government and the administration is under their control and supervision. In the Parliamentary system, the legislature also exercises control over the administration. The administrative officers cannot act in violation of the policies adopted by the legislature and the machinery is also made politically accountable.

17. How bureaucracy is important for the political system of a country?

Ans. Bureaucracy is responsible to carry out and implement the policies of the government. Good policies and laws can really serve their objectives only when there are efficiently implemented by the civil servants. Political neutrality is also expected of the bureaucracy, this implies that the bureaucracy will refrain from taking stance on policy issues. Policy-making is the function of the political executive.

However, the bureaucracy plays an active role in this exercise. Civil servants supply the data needed by the political executive for formulating the policies. It run the day-to-day administration in accordance with the policies, laws, rules and regulation of the government. It also advice the political executive. Thus, bureaucracy is important for the political system of a country.

• Long Answer Type Questions

1. Describe the various forms of the government in details.

Ans. The various forms of government are

Presidential System In the Presidential system; the office of the President is very powerful both in theory and practice as the President is the head of the state as well as the head of the government. In this System, the President is directly elected by the people and he is not answerable to the legislature. For example, USA, Brazil, etc. opted for presidential form of government.

Parliamentary System The system in which the formulation of policies and enactment of the laws are done by the Parliament is called Parliamentary system. In this system, the Prime Minister is the real head of the government, while the President or Monarch is the nominal head of the state. For example, UK, Portugal, etc. opted for parliamentary form of government.

Semi-Presidential System This is the form of government which has both the President and Prime Minister, where the President is the head of the state and Prime Minister is head of the government, with his council responsible to the legislature. But, unlike the parliamentary system, the President may possess significant day-to-day powers. It is possible that the President and Prime Minister belong to the same party and at times belong to different parties. For example, Russia, Sri Lanka, etc. opted for Semi-Presidential form of government.

2. Why does India opt for Parliamentary form of government?

Ans. India choose the parliamentary form of government because.

  (i) Being a British colony, India was influenced by the British Parliamentary System of governance.

  (ii) To give equal importance to the multiple religious and groups so that they could elect their representatives.

  (iii) In the parliamentary system the executives are controlled by the representative of people. Thus, it reduces the chances of dictatorship.

  (iv) When the Constitution of India was written, India already had some experience of running the parliamentary system under the Government of India Act, 1919 and 1935.

  (v) The maker of the Indian Constitution wanted to ensure that the government would be sensitive to public expectation and would be responsible and accountable.

India had the alternative of presidential form of government which puts much emphasis on the President as the Chief Executive and source of all executive power. But it always poses a danger of personality cult in Presidential Executive. So, the makers of the Indian Constitution in order to provide enough safeguards to check against the personality cult, adopted the parliamentary form of government both at the centre and state level.

According to the parliamentary form of government, the President (a formal Head of the State) and the Prime Minister with his Council of Ministers comprises the executive at the national level, whereas the Governor and the Chief Minister with his Council of Ministers comprises the executive at the state level to run the government.

3. What are the three situations, where the President exercise his discretionary power? State the discretionary powers of the President.

Ans. There are three situations where the President exercises his discretionary powers

  (i) **Firstly**, when the President thinks that the advice rendered to him has certain flaws or legal breakdown, it is not in the best interest of the country, then the President can ask the Council of Ministers to reconsider the decision. However, if the Council of Ministers send back the same advice, then the President would be bound to consider that advice or decision.

  (ii) **Secondly**, every bill passed by the Parliament goes to the President for his assent to become law. The President can send the bill back for reconsideration and if the bill is sent back to the President for the second time, then the President is bound to give assent to the bill as his veto power is limited. The President can just keep the bill pending with him without any time limit and enjoys informal power to use this veto in effective manner which is referred to as 'Pocket Veto'.

  (iii) **Thirdly**, in a situation after election when no leader has acquired majority in the Lok Sabha to form Government, then the President exercises his discretion in judging who really may have the support of the majority or who can actually form and run the government. However, this discretion comes out of political circumstances.

However, this discretion comes out of political circumstances. In ordinary circumstances, if the Council of Ministers are removed as they depend on the support of the majority in legislature, then the President has the power to make a choice in appointing the Prime Minister to run the government of the country.

4. What is the tenure of the Prime Minister? Also write the power and functions of the Prime Minister?

Ans. The tenure of the Prime Minister is not fixed, he holds office during the pleasure of the President. The Prime Minister loses his office if the majority is lost. Formally, a leader who has the support of majority is appointed by the President as Prime Minister and then the Prime Minister decides the Council of Ministers.

In India, the Prime Minister enjoys a pre-eminent place in the government by following ways

- The allocation of ranks and portfolios to the ministers is done by the Prime Minister depending upon the seniority and political importance. The ranks of Cabinet Minister or Minister of State or Deputy Minister are assigned by the Prime Minister and the same is done by the Chief Minister in the state level government.

- The Council of Ministers comes into existence only after the Prime Minister has taken oath of office, hence, the Council of Ministers cannot exist without the Prime Minister.

- The death or resignation of the Prime Minister automatically dissolves the Council of Ministers but the death, dismissal, resignation of minister only creates a ministerial vacancy.

- The Prime Minister acts as a link between the Council of Ministers on one hand and the President and Parliament together on the other hand.

- It is constitutionally mandatory for the Prime Minister to communicate to the President all decisions of the Council of Ministers relating to the administrative affair of the Union and proposals of legislation. The Prime Minister is involved in all crucial decisions of the government and decides on the policies of the government.

Thus, the power exercised by the Prime Minister flows from various sources, such as, control over the Council of Ministers, leadership of Lok Sabha, command over bureaucratic machinery, etc.

5. What do you mean coalition government? How it has affected the working of the parliamentary executive?

Ans. A coalition government is a cabinet of a parliamentary government in which multiple political parties co-operate, reducing the dominance of any one party within that coalition. The usual reason given for this arrangement is that no party on its own achieve a majority in the Parliament.

The system of coalition government in India is prevalent since 1989 but many such governments could not remain in power for the full term of Lok Sabha.

These developments have affected the working of the parliamentary executive in following ways

- It resulted in growing discretionary role of the President in selection of the Prime Minister.

- The coalition nature of Indian politics, has necessitated much more consultation between political partners, leading to erosion of prime ministerial authority.

- It has also brought restrictions on the privileges of the Prime Minister, like choosing the ministers and deciding their ranks and portfolios.

- The policies and programmes of the government cannot be decided by the Prime Minister alone, as the political parties of different ideologies come together to form government.

- It has led to a lot of negotiations and compromises in policy formulation.

• Case Based Questions

1. Read the passage and answer the questions that follows.

In this system, there are mechanisms that ensure that the executive will be answerable to and controlled by the legislature or people's representatives. The President and the Prime Minister with his Council of Ministers comprises the executive at the national level, whereas, the Governor and the Chief Minister with his Council of Ministers comprises the executive at the state level to run the government.

(i) Who is the nominal head in the Parliamentary System of Government?

(ii) What is the composition of the executive at the National and State level?

(iii) Which type of the system of government the above passage talking about? Why does India follow this system of government?

Ans. (i) In the Parliamentary system of government the President is the nominal head of the state and the real head is the Prime Minister.

(ii) The President and the Prime Minister with his Council of Ministers comprises the executive at the national level, whereas, the Governor and the Chief Minister with his Council of Ministers comprises the executive at the state level.

(iii) The above passage is talking about Parliamentary form of Government. India follows Parliamentary system of government because India already had some experience of running the Parliamentary system under the Government of India's Act, 1919 and 1935.

2. Read the following source and answer the questions that follows.

The Indian bureaucracy today is an enormously complex system. It consists of the All India Services, State Services, employees of the local governments and technical and managerial staff running public sector undertakings. Makers of our Constitution were aware of the importance of the non-partisan and professional bureaucracy. They also wanted the members of the civil services or bureaucracy to be impartially selected on the basis of merit. So, the Union Public Service Commission has been entrusted with the task of conducting the process of recruitment of the civil servants for the Government of India. Similar Public Service Commissions are provided for the States also. Members of the Public Service Commissions are appointed for a fixed term. Their removal or suspension is subject to a thorough enquiry made by a Judge of the Supreme Court.

(i) What is called as Permanent Executive?

(ii) What is the selection procedure to appoint the Bureaucrats?

(iii) What is the tenure of the members of the Public Service Commission?

Ans. (i) Permanent executive i.e. Bureaucracy or administrative machinery is one of the executive organs of the government who works as a permanent employee and are assigned the task of assisting the ministries in formulating policies and implementing these policies.

(ii) The selection procedure to the members of civil services of bureaucracy is impartially selected on the basis of merit by the Union Public Service Commission (UPSC) at the centre and the similar Public Service Commission is provided for the states also.

(iii) Members of the Public Service Commissions are appointed for a fixed term of six years or until the attainment of sixty- five years of age in the case of Union Public Service Commission and sixty-two years in the case of State Public Service Commission.

3. Observe the cartoon given below and answer the questions that follow.

(i) What does the cartoon represents and what message does the cartoon convey?

(ii) Mention the function of the Prime Minister in relation with the Council of Ministers?

(iii) How is the Council of Ministers appointed??

Ans. (i) The cartoon represents the Council of Ministers headed by the Prime Minister. The cartoon conveys the message that the Prime Minister is the head of the Council of Ministers and it is bound by the words of Prime Minister.

(ii) The functions of Prime Minister in relation to the Council of Ministers are

   • The council comes into existence only after the Prime Minister has taken the oath of office.

   • The death or resignation of the Prime Minister automatically dissolves the Council of Ministers.

(iii) The Council of Ministers are appointed by the President on the advice of the Prime Minister.

4. Observe the cartoon given below and answer the questions that follow.

(i) Why do people want to be ministers?

(ii) This cartoon seems to suggest that it is only for perks and status. Then, why is there a competition for some portfolios?

(iii) What is 'portfolio'? Why is the minister unhappy with the portfolio??

Ans. (i) The people want to be ministers for gaining the advantage of perks and status.

(iii) There is a competition for some portfolios for better status, more powers, extra earnings and for more importance among the people and their leaders.

(iii) Portfolio refers to the position and duties of a minister. Ministers are assigned portfolios or ministries depending upon the seniority and political importance. The Minister is unhappy with the portfolio because it does not cover the perks and status of the minister.

Chapter Test

- **Objective Type Questions**

  1 In which among the following countries, Parliamentary system is followed?
     (a) Italy   (b) Sri Lanka   (c) Brazil   (d) Russia

  2 Who among the following acts as Ex-office Chairman of Rajya Sabha?
     (a) President   (b) Leader of opposition (c) Vice-President (d) Prime Minister

  3 The Body responsible for the day to day administration is called .... Executive.
     (a) Permanent   (b) Political   (c) Social   (d) None of these

  4 Which of the following government organs is responsible for the implementation of rules and regulation?
     (i) Legislature   (ii) Judiciary   (iii) Executive   (iv) Bureaucracy
     Select the correct options.
     (a) Only (i)   (b) (iii) and (ii)   (c) (iii) and (iv)   (d) Only (iii)

- **Short Answer Type Questions**

  1 Distinguish between parliamentary executive and presidential executive.
  2 Discuss the relationship between Governor and the State Council of Ministers.
  3 Mention the discretionary powers of the President.
  4 How bureaucracy is important for the political system of a country?
  5 Why was parliamentary system adopted in India?
  6 Write a short note on Council of Ministers.

- **Long Answer Type Questions**

  1 Describe the role of civil services in administration.
  2 Critically examine the emergency powers of the President.
  3 Mention the powers and functions of the Prime Ministers.

Judiciary

In this Chapter...
- Need of an Independent Judiciary
- Judiciary and Rights
- Judicial Activism
- Judiciary and Parliament

The judiciary is the system of courts that interprets the laws and perform some political functions also. Judiciary is an important organ of the government and the **Supreme Court of India** is one of the most powerful court in the world. It plays an important role in interpreting and protecting the **Fundamental Rights** of the citizens.

Need of an Independent Judiciary

The judiciary provides a mechanism for the resolution of disputes arising in any society between groups, and between individuals or groups and government, in accordance with the **principle of rule of law**. The idea of rule of law implies that all individuals whether rich or poor, men or women, forward or backward castes are subjected to the same law.

Need of the Independent Judiciary arises due to the following reasons

- The principal role of judiciary is to protect the rule of law and ensure **supremacy of law**.
- It **safeguards the rights of the individual** and settles disputes in accordance with the law.
- It ensures that **democracy** does not give way to any sort of **dictatorship**.
- In order to be able to do all this, judiciary has to be independent from political pressure.

Independence of Judiciary

In order to enable judiciary to perform its functions effectively, it is necessary that judiciary is kept independent of any outside interference.

Independence of judiciary means that

- The executive and legislature must not restrict the functioning of the judiciary in such a way that it is unable to deliver justice.
- The other organs of perform their the government should not interfere with the decisions of the judiciary.
- Judges must be able to perform their function without any fear or favour.

Independence of judiciary does not imply arbitrariness or absence of accountability. Judiciary is also the part of democratic political structure of the country and therefore, accountable to the constitution and to the people of the country.

Means to Provide and Protect Independence of Judiciary

The Constitution of India has ensured the independence of judiciary through various measures

- The legislature is not involved in the process of appointment of judges. Thus, party politics is not involved in the process of appointments. A person must have experience as a lawyer and /or must be well versed in law, to be appointed as a judge. Political opinions of the person or his/her political loyalty should not be the criteria for appointments to judiciary.
- The judges have a fixed tenure of office till reaching the age of retirement. Security of tenure ensures that they function without fear or favour.

- The Constitution prescribes a very difficult procedure for the removal of judges in order to provide security of tenure to the members of the judiciary.
- The judiciary is not financially dependent on either the executive or legislature. The salaries and allowances of the judges are not subjected to the approval of the legislature.
- The actions and decisions of the judges are immune from personal criticism and the judiciary has the power to penalise those who are guilty of contempt of court.
- Parliament cannot discuss the conduct of judges except when the proceeding for removal is carried out.

Appointment of Judges

The appointment of judges is a part of the political process. Council of Ministers, Governors and Chief Ministers and Chief Justice of India all influence the process of judicial appointment. According to the convention the senior most judge of the Supreme Court is appointed as the **Chief Justice of India** (CJI).

However, this convention was broken twice. In 1973, **AN Ray** was appointed as CJI superseding three senior Judges. Again, **Justice MH Beg** was appointed superseding **Justice HR Khanna** (1975).

The other Judges of the Supreme Court and the High Court are appointed by the President after consultation with the CJI. This, in effect, meant that the final decisions in matters of appointment rested with Council of Ministers.

Between 1982 and 1998, the Supreme Court heard several cases during this time. Initially, the court considered the Chief Justice's role to be purely advisory in nature.

Then it took the view that the opinion of the Chief Justice must be followed by the President. Finally, the Supreme Court has proposed a novel procedure the Chief Justice should recommend names of people to be appointed after consulting with four senior most judges of the court. Thus, the Supreme Court has established the principle of collegium in making recommendations for appointments.

As, a result, in matters of appointment, the Supreme Court's opinion of a group of senior judges carries more weight. Thus, the Supreme Court and the Council of Ministers play an important role in appointing judges.

Removal of Judges

A judge of Supreme Court or High Court can be removed only on grounds of **proved misbehaviour** or **incapacity**. A motion containing the charges against the judges must be approved by **special majority** in both the Houses of the Parliament.

The procedure for the removal of judges is very difficult and unless there is general consensus among Members of Parliament, a judge cannot be removed.

The **executive** plays a crucial role in appointment process, while the **legislature** has the powers of removal. This ensures both balance of power and independence of the judiciary.

> ### Unsuccessful Attempt to Remove a Judge
>
> In 1991, 108 members of Parliament signed the first-ever resolution to remove a Supreme Court Justice. V. Ramaswami, during his tenure as the Chief Justice of the Punjab and Haryana High Court was accused of misappropriating funds.
>
> The motion recommending his removal got the required two-thirds majority among the members who were present and voting, but the Congress party abstained from voting in the House. Therefore, the motion could not get the support of one-half of the total strength of the House.

Structure of the Judiciary

The Constitution of India provides for a single integrated judicial system. The structure of judiciary in India is **pyramidal** with Supreme Court at the top, High Courts below them and district and subordinate courts at the lowest level. The lower courts function under the direct superintendence of the higher courts.

Structure of judiciary is given below

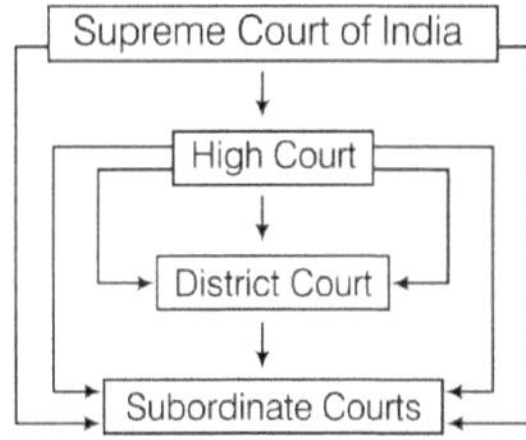

Supreme Court of India

- It is the highest court of appeal.
- Its decisions are binding on all courts.
- Can transfer judges of High Courts.
- Can move cases from any court to itself.

High Court

- Can hear appeal from lower courts.
- Can issue writs for enforcing Fundamental Rights.
- Exercises suprintendence and control over courts below it.
- Deals with cases within the concerned state jurisdiction.

District Court

- Deals with cases arising in the district.
- Considers appeals on decisions given by lower courts.
- Decides cases involving serious criminal offences.

Subordinate Courts

These courts consider the cases of civil and criminal nature.

Jurisdiction of Supreme Court

The Supreme Court of India is one of the most powerful court in the world. However, it functions within the limitations imposed by the constitution. The Supreme Court has specific jurisdiction or scope of powers.

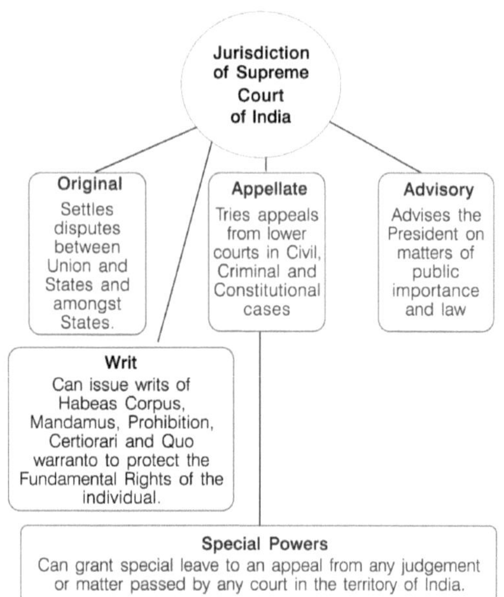

Jurisdictions of Supreme Court

Original Jurisdiction

Original jurisdiction means cases that can be directly considered by the Supreme Court without going to the lower courts before that. In any federal country, legal disputes are bound to arise between union and the states and among the states themselves.

The power to resolve such cases is entrusted to Supreme Court of India. It is called **original jurisdiction** because Supreme Court alone has the power to deal with such cases. Neither the High Court nor the lower courts has the power to deal with such cases. The Supreme Court not just settles disputes but also interprets the power of Union and State government as laid down in the constitution.

Writ Jurisdiction

In case of violation of the Fundamental Rights, the individual can approach the Supreme Court directly. It give special orders to be followed in the form of writs. This jurisdiction is known as **writ jurisdiction**. The High Court can also issue writs, but the persons whose rights are violated have the choice of either approaching the High Court or approaching Supreme Court.

Appellate Jurisdiction

The Supreme Court is the highest court of **appeal**. Appellate jurisdiction means that the Supreme Court will reconsider the decisions made by the High Court in the constitutional matters and decisions made by the lower court involving death sentence or criminal matters, etc. However, the High Court must certify that the case is fit for appeal and the Supreme Court holds the power to decide whether to admit appeals even when appeal is not allowed by High Court.

The Supreme Court can change the ruling and along with that also give new interpretation of provision involved, if it find necessary. The High Courts too, have appellate jurisdiction over the decision given by courts below them.

Advisory Jurisdiction

The Supreme Court of India possesses advisory jurisdiction, which means that the President of India has the authority to refer any matter of public interest or involving constitutional interpretation to the Supreme Court for advice. The Supreme Court, on the other hand, is not bound to provide advice on such matter, and the President is not bound to take such advice.

The utility of the advisory jurisdictions of Supreme Court is two fold

(i) It allows the government to seek Legal opinion on a matter of importance before taking action on it. This may prevent unneccessary litigations later.

(ii) The government can make suitable changes in its actions of legislation in the light of the advice of Supreme Court.

Decisions made by Supreme Court are binding on other courts within the territory of India and are also enforceable throughout the length and breadth of the country. The Supreme Court itself is not bound by its decision and can review it anytime as prescribed by the provisions of the constitution.

Article 137 of Constitution states that the Supreme Court shall have power to review any judgement pronounced or order made by it.

Article 144 states that all authorities, civil and judicial, in territory of India shall act in aid of Supreme Court.

Judiciary and Rights

Judiciary is entrusted with the task of protecting the rights of individuals and the Supreme Court can remedy the violation of rights in two ways as provided by the constitution

(i) **Article 32** states that, it can restore Fundamentqal Rights by issuing various writs. The **High Court** also have the power to issue writs which comes under **Article 226**.

(ii) According to **Article 13** the Supreme Court can declare the concerned law as unconstitutional and therefore, non-operational. This involves **Judicial Review**.

Judicial Review

Judicial Review means the power of Supreme Court and High Courts to examine the constitutionality of any law. If the Court arrives at the conclusion that the law is inconsistent with the provisions of the constitution, such law is declared **unconstitutional** and **void**. Together, the writ powers and the judicial review power of the court make judiciary very powerful.

The word 'judicial review' no where mentioned in the Constitution. The fact that India has a written constitution and that the Supreme Court has the power to strike down a law that violate Constitutional Rights implies that the Supreme Court has the power of judicial review.

Furthermore, as we saw in the section on Supreme Court jurisdiction, the Supreme Court can use its review powers in the case of federal relations if a law is inconsistent with the distribution of powers laid down by the constitution.

Suppose, the Central Government makes a law, which according to some states, concerns a subject from State List. The states will then take their case to the Supreme Court, and if the court agrees with them, it would declare that the law is unconstitutional.

In this context, the Supreme Court's review power provides the ability to examine laws on the basis of whether it violates human rights or the federal power distribution. The right of review applies to legislation enacted by State Legislatures as well. In particular, the review power means that the judiciary can **interpret the constitution** and the laws passed by the legislature.

The practice of entertaining PILs has further added to the powers of the judiciary in protecting rights of citizen.

Judicial Activism

Judicial activism or **Public Interest Litigation** (PIL) or **Social Action Litigation** (SAL) have revolutionised the functioning of judiciary and made it more people friendly. PIL is the **chief instrument** through which judicial activism has flourished in India. A person whose rights have been violated or who is involved in a dispute, could move to the court of law. This concept underwent a change around 1979.

In 1979, a person filed a case in court on behalf of the aggrieved person of society on the matters of public interest and not for personal benefit. Such a case is known as Public Interest Litigation.

Supreme Court also took up the case about rights of prisoners. This opened the gates for large number of cases where citizens and voluntary organisations sought judicial intervention for protection of existing rights, betterment of life conditions of poor, protection of the environment and many other issues in the interest of the public. For example, **Husainara Khatoon** *vs* **Bihar Case** (1979) about under traits and **Sunil Batra** *vs* **Delhi Administration** (1980).

PIL has become the most important tool of judicial activism. Judiciary can consider cases on the basis of newspaper reports and postal complaints received by the court. Thus, the role of judiciary became more popular by judicial activism.

Impact of Judicial Activism

Impact of judicial activism can be positive as well as negative

Positive Impact

- Democratisation of judicial system by allowing groups as well as individual to enter the courts.
- It has forced executive accountability. It has also attempted to make the electoral system more accessible and transparent.
- The court asked candidate contesting elections to file affidavits detailing their properties, wages and educational qualifications so that voters could elect their representatives based on accurate information.

Negative Impact

- PIL has over burdened the courts.
- Judicial activism has blurred the line of distinction between the executive and legislature on one hand and the judiciary on the other.
- The court is involved in resolving the questions which belongs to executive such as, reducing air or sound pollution or investigating cases of corruption or bringing about electoral reforms, which is not exactly the duty of judiciary.
- Democratic principle has being strained because of judicial activism.

Judicial Overreach

When judiciary assumes the roles and functions of the legislature and executive, thus diluting the concept of separation of powers, it becomes judicial overreach. Unrestrained activism on the part of judiciary often leads to its overreach. When a court goes beyond of its authority and interferes in areas that are under the control of the executive and/or legislative, it is known as Judicial overreach.

It indicates the Court has broken the theory of **separation of powers by** taking on tasks such as law enforcement, policymaking or law making or interfering in the executive's day-to-day operations. This is a scenario in which a court exceeds its legal authority as defined by the constitution and other legal documents. The executive's function is also encroached upon by the courts, which make executive decisions.

For example, judiciary can introduce policies which are the domain of the legislature and can lay down regulations which are the domain of the executive. The Supreme Court has **discretionary power** under **Article 142**, which specifies that in the exercise of its jurisdiction, the court may pass any decree or make any order required to complete justice in any case or issue pending before it.

Power of Supreme Court and **Article 142** of Constitution have been put to many constructive uses. But there is still need for judicial restraints in the exercise of judicial review because **National Judicial Appointment Commission** (NJAC) was declared unconstitutional as it tried to apply check on judicial power.

Judiciary and Parliament

The court has been active in seeking to prevent subversion of the constitution through political practice. Thus, areas beyond the scope of Judicial Review such as powers of President and Governor were brought under the purview of courts.

The Indian Constitution is based on the principle of limited **separation of powers** and **checks and balances**[1], which means that each organ of the government has a clear area of functioning. The Parliament is supreme in law making and amending the constitution, the executive is supreme in implementing them while the judiciary is supreme in settling disputes and deciding whether the law that have been made are in accordance with the provisions of the Constitution.

There has always been controversies arising on the floor regarding the contentious issues between the legislature and judiciary such as land reform laws, laws enforcing preventive detention, laws governing reservation in jobs, restrictions over right to property, etc.

This debate erupted into a full-fledged war between 1967 and 1973. Apart from land reform laws, there have been conflicts between the legislature and the judiciary over laws enforcing preventive detention, laws governing job reservations, regulations acquiring private property for public purposes, and laws determining compensation for such acquisitions of private property.

For instance, the Supreme Court's decision in the famous case of **Keshavananda Bharti case in 1973**, is very important in regulating the relation between legislature and judiciary. The court ruled that there is the **basic structure of the constitution** that cannot be violated, even by the Parliament.

Further, the court rules out two more things, firstly, it declared that right to property is not a part of basic structure and could be suitably abridged (abstracted). Secondly, the court reserved to itself the right to decide whether the matters are a part of the basic structure or not.

This ruling has changed the nature of conflicts between the legistature and judiciary.

---

1. **Checks and Balances** The system of Checks and Balances is an important part of the constitution. With check and Balances each of the three branches of government (Legislature, Executive and Judiciary) can limit the powers of others.

Chapter Practice

Objective Questions

• Multiple Choice Questions

1. Which of the following government organs provides a mechanism for the resolution of disputes between individuals or private parties?

(a) Legislature   (b) Judiciary

(c) Executive   (d) Bureaucracy

Ans. (b) The judiciary is an important organ of the government. It provides a mechanism for the resolution of disputes between individuals or private parties.

2. Which of the following is not a principal function of judiciary? **[NCERT]**

(a) Ensure supremacy of law

(b) Protect Fundamental Right of individual

(c) Settle disputes

(d) Promote personality cult

Ans. (d) The principal function of judiciary is to protect the rule of law, ensure supremacy of law, safeguards the rights of the individual and settles disputes in accordance with the law. Hence (d) is the correct option.

3. Judiciary ensures that democracy does not give way to any sort of ....

(i) Dictatorship   (ii) Totalitarianism

(iii) Authoritarianism

Select the correct code.

(a) Only (i)   (b) (ii) and (iii)

(c) (i) and (iii)   (d) All of these

Ans. (d) All of these are the correct option because they all are similar to Dictatorship.

4. Which of the following organ of the government is not involved in the process of appointment of judges?

(a) Executive   (b) Legislature

(c) Judiciary   (d) None of these

Ans. (b) Judges are appointed by the collegium system which consist of Chief Justice and the four seniors most judges and collegium forward the name of the persons for appointment to the government i.e., the Executive. Hence, Legislature is not involved.

5. Consider the following statements related to Judges

(i) The judges have a fixed tenure of office till reaching the age of retirement.

(ii) The salaries and allowances of the judges are subjected to the approval of the legislature.

Select the correct code.

(a) Only (i)

(b) Only (ii)

(c) Both (i) and (ii)

(d) None of the above

Ans. (a) The Constitution of India has given fixed tenure to the Judges so that they can function smoothly. Hence, statement (i) is correct.

The salaries and allowances of the judges are not subjected to the approval of the legislature. Hence statement (ii) is incorrect. Therefore (a) is the correct option.

6. Who among the following does not influence the process of judicial appointment?

(a) Chief Justice of India

(b) Council of Ministers

(c) President

(d) Bar Council of India

Ans. (d) Supreme Court and the Council of Ministers play an important role in appointing judges. Hence (d) is the correct option.

7. Under collegium system of judicial appointment how many seniors most judges are consulted apart from Chief Justice?

(a) Four   (b) Five   (c) Six   (d) Two

Ans. (a) The Collegium comprises of the Chief Justice and four senior most judges.

8. The .... plays a crucial role in appointment process, while the .... has the powers of removal?

(a) President, executive

(b) Executive, Legislature

(c) Legislature, executive

(d) Speaker, Vice-Chairman

Ans. (b) The Executive plays a crucial role in appointment process, while the Legislature has the powers of removal.

9. Consider the following statements related to the High Courts.

(i) It can hear appeal from lower courts.

(ii) It cannot issue writs for enforcing Fundamental Rights.

Select the correct statements.

(a) Only (i)   (b) Only (ii)

(c) Both (i) and (ii)   (d) None of these

Ans. (a) Under Article 226 of the Constitution High Court has the power to issue writs for the violation of Fundamental Right. Hence, statement (ii) is incorrect.

High Court can hear appeals from the lower courts. Hence, statement (i) is correct. Therefore (a) is the correct option.

10. Who has the power to deal cases that are arising between Union and the States and among the states themselves?

(a) Civil Court

(b) District Court

(c) Supreme Court

(d) High Court

Ans. (c) The power to resolve such cases is entrusted to the Supreme Court of India. It is called original jurisdiction because it alone has the power to deal with such cases. Neither the High Court nor the lower courts have the power to deal with such cases.

11. Consider the following statements related to advisory jurisdiction of the Supreme Court?

(i) The Supreme Court, is obligated to provide advice on such matter as referred by the President.

(ii) President is obligated to take such advice.

Select the correct statements.

(a) Only (i)   (b) Only (ii)

(c) Both (i) and (ii)   (d) None of these

Ans. (d) The Supreme Court of India possesses advisory jurisdiction which means if any matter is referred by the President to the Supreme Court, the court is not obligated to provide advice on such matter as referred by the President. Hence statement (i) is incorrect. President is not obligated to take such advice. Hence statement (ii) is incorrect. Therefore (d) is the correct option.

12. Public Interest Litigations has become the most important vehicle of ....

(a) Judicial Review   (b) Judicial Activism

(c) Judicial Overreach   (d) None of these

Ans. (b) Public Interest Litigations has become the most important vehicle of Judicial Activism.

13. Consider the following statements.

(i) Social Action Litigation (SAL) have revolutionised the functioning of judiciary and made it more people friendly.

(ii) PIL is the chief instrument through which judicial review has flourished in India.

Select the correct statements.

(a) Only (i)   (b) Only (ii)

(c) Both (i) and (ii)   (d) None of these

Ans. (a) Social Action Litigation (SAL) have revolutionised the functioning of judiciary and made it more people friendly. Hence statement (i) is correct.

PIL is the chief instrument through which judicial activism has flourished in India. Hence statement (ii) is incorrect. Therefore (a) is the correct option.

14. When a court goes beyond of its authority and interferes in areas that are under the control of the executive or legislative, it is known as ....

(a) Judicial Activism

(b) Judicial Review

(c) Judicial Overreach

(d) Public Litigation Interest

Ans. (c) When a court goes beyond of its authority and interferes in areas that are under the control of the executive or legislative, it is known as Judicial Overreach.

15. In which year did the Supreme Court gave judgement in Keshvananda Bharti Case?

(a) 1971   (b) 1973

(c) 1975   (d) 1977

Ans. (b) The Supreme Court's decision in the famous case of Keshavananda Bharti Case in 1973, is very important in regulating the relation between Legislature and Judiciary. The court ruled that there is the basic structure of the constitution that cannot be violated, even by the Parliament.

• Assertion-Reasoning MCQs

Directions (Q. Nos. 16-20) In the question given below, there are two statements marked as Assertion (A) and Reason (R). Read the statements and choose the correct options.

Codes

(a) Both A and R are true and R is the correct explanation of A.

(b) Both A and R are true, but R is not the correct explanation of A.

(c) A is true, but R is false.

(d) A is false, but R is true.

16. Assertion (A) The judiciary provides a mechanism for the resolution of disputes arising in any society between groups or individuals.

Reason (R) The Supreme Court has the original jurisdiction.

Ans. (a) Both the statements A and R are correct and R is the correct explanation of A. Since the Supreme Court has the original jurisdiction so it can provide a mechanism for the resolution of disputes arising in any society between groups or individual.

17. Assertion (A) In India, the judiciary is independent of the executive.

Reason (R) Judiciary favours the government and helps in the implementation of its plans.

Ans. (d) In India, the judiciary is completely independent of the executive. It has no interference in the affairs of the state nor can it be influenced by the government. Hence, option (d) is correct.

18. Assertion (A) The Constitution of India provides for a single integrated judicial system.

Reason (R) Supreme Court decisions are binding precedent for lower subordinate courts.

Ans. (a) Both A and R are correct and R is the correct explanation of A.

19. Assertion (A) The role of judiciary became more popular by judicial activism.

Reason (R) Judiciary can consider cases on the basis of newspaper reports and postal complaints received by the court.

Ans. (a) Both the statements A and R are correct and R is the correct explanation of A. Since the judiciary has the power to consider cases on the basis of newspaper report as a result of this the role of judiciary become more popular.

20. Assertion (A) Judicial activism fills the gap, since the existing law is not clear or pronounced.

Reason (R) Judicial activism emerged in India as an extra constitutional development through judicial pronouncements and judgements.

Ans. (b) Both the statements A and R are correct and R is not the correct explanation of A. Judicial activism fills the gap, since the existing law is not clear or pronounced is the reason. In this it is vice-versa.

• Case Based MCQs

1. Read the passage and answer the questions that follow.

The judges have a fixed tenure. They hold office till reaching the age of retirement. Only in exceptional cases, judges may be removed. But otherwise, they have security of tenure. Security of tenure ensures that judges could function without fear or favour. The Constitution prescribes a very difficult procedure for removal of judges. The Constitution makers believed that a difficult procedure of removal would provide security of office to the members of judiciary.

(i) The judiciary is not financially dependent on ....

(a) Executive   (b) Legislature
(c) Both (a) and (b)   (d) Neither (a) nor (b)

Ans. (c) The salaries of the judges are not varied i.e., not decided by the Legislature or the Executive. Hence, they are not financial dependent on them.

(ii) The other Judges of the Supreme Court and the High Court are appointed by the .... after 'consulting' the CJI.

(a) Chief Minister   (b) President
(c) Governor   (d) Prime Minister

Ans. (b) The Judges are appointed by the President but the Collegium selects the judges who then forward names to the Central Government.

(iii) On what grounds does the Judge of Supreme Court and High Court be removed?

(a) Misbehaviour   (b) Incapacity
(c) Both (a) and (b)   (d) Neither (a) nor (b)

Ans. (c) The is only two grounds for the removal of the Judges i.e., misbehaviour or incapacity.

(iv) What is the retirement age of the Judges of the Supreme Court?

(a) 62 years   (b) 65 years
(c) 60 years   (d) 70 years

Ans. (b) The retirement age of the judges of the Supreme Court is 65 years whereas for the High Court it is 62 years.

(v) Consider the following statements.

1. All the Judges in India have same fixed tenure.
2. There is no ground mentioned in the Constitution of India for the removal of the Judges.

Which of the following is/are true?

(a) Only 1   (b) Only 2
(c) Both 1 and 2   (d) Neither 1 nor 2

Ans. (d) At present, the retirement age is 65 years for Supreme Court Judges and 62 years for High Court Judges. Hence, statement 1 is incorrect.

The judges can be removed on two grounds i.e., if proved misbehaviour and incapacity. Hence statement 2 is incorrect. Therefore (d) is the correct answer.

PART 2
Subjective Questions

• Short Answer Type Questions

1. Explain in brief the meaning of Independence of judiciary.

Ans. Independence of judiciary means that

- The executive and legislature must not restrict the functioning of judiciary.
- The other organs of the government should not interfere with the decisions of the judiciary.
- Judges must be able to function without any fear or favour.

Independence of judiciary does not imply anti-democratic or absence of accountability. The judiciary has to work in accordance with the Indian Constitution. Judiciary is also the part of democratic political structure of the country and therefore, accountable to the constitution and people of the country.

2. What are the different provisions in the Constitution in order to maintain the independence of judiciary? **[NCERT]**

Ans. The different provisions in the constitution in order to maintain the independence of judiciary are

- The conduct of judges cannot be discussed in the Parliament.
- The Legislature is not involved in the process of appointment of judges.
- The judges have fixed tenure that ensures that they can work without fear and favour. They can be removed only in exceptional cases. The procedure for the removal of judges of Supreme Court and High Court is extremely difficult.
- The approval of the Legislature is not required for salaries and allowances of the judges.
- The instructions of the judiciary have to be followed by the legislature and executive of the country.

3. Discuss the role of judiciary in context of the rights. **[NCERT]**

Ans. Right from 1950 the judiciary has played an important role in interpreting and in protecting the Constitution.

Judiciary is entrusted with the task of protecting the rights of individuals and the Supreme Court or High Court can protect the violation of rights in two ways as provided by the Constitution

(i) It can restore Fundamental Rights by issuing various writs.

(ii) The Supreme Court can declare the concerned law unconstitutional and therefore, non-operational.

The second of the two ways involves Judicial Review, which means the power of the Supreme Court to examine the constitutionality of any law, if the court arrives at the conclusion that the law is inconsistent with the provision of the constitution.

4. What is the procedure for the removal of the judges?

Ans. The removal of judges of the Supreme Court and the High Courts is also extremely difficult. A Judge of the Supreme Court or High Court can be removed only on the ground of proven misbehaviour or incapacity. A motion containing the charges against the judge must be approved by special majority i.e. (majority of total membership of that house and by a majority of not less than two-thirds of the members of that house present and voting) in both Houses of the Parliament.

It is clear from this procedure and unless there is a general consensus among Members of Parliament, a judge cannot be removed. It should also be noted that while in making appointments, the Executive plays a crucial role; the legislature has the powers of removal.

5. Has there any attempt made in Indian Judiciary to remove the Judges of the Supreme Court?

Ans. In 1991 the first-ever motion to remove a Supreme Court Justice was signed by 108 Members of Parliament. Justice V. Ramaswami, during his tenure as the Chief Justice of the Punjab and Haryana High Court was accused of misappropriating funds. The motion recommending his removal got the required two-thirds majority among the members who were present and voting, but the Congress party abstained from voting in the House.

Therefore, the motion could not get the support of one-half of the total strength of the House.

6. What is the importance of judiciary in India? **[NCERT]**

Ans. Judiciary plays an important role in imparting justice to people. It also performs the following functions

- The judiciary act as the guardian of the constitution by interpreting it in a proper manner as it can declare any law passed by legislature unconstitutional, if it is inconsistent with the Constitution.
- The judiciary performs administrative functions by keeping check on the functioning of each court.
- The judiciary act as the protector of Fundamental Rights in case of its violation and issue orders for its implementation.
- The judiciary performs legislative functions by giving judgements and making laws to fill up the gap between the legislature and society.

7. When does the Supreme Court of India advises the President? Is that advice binding on him?

Ans. Under Article 143 of the Constitution, the Supreme Court exercises advisory or consultative functions also. Article 143 provides that if any time it appears to the President that a question of law has arisen or is likely to arise which is of public importance, he may refer the matter to the Supreme Court for consideration and opinion. Such a question is heard by a bench consisting of atleast five judges and the court follows the procedure of an ordinary trial. The majority opinion is sent to the President. The judges can hold dissenting opinion as well.

The opinion of the Supreme Court is not binding on the President as it is not of the nature of a judicial pronouncement. Nor is it obligatory for the Supreme Court to give its opinion.

8. Do you think judicial activism can lead to conflict between judiciary and executive? **[NCERT]**

Ans. Judicial activism can lead to conflict between the judiciary and the executive because of the interference of the judiciary in the domain of the executive. Issues related to pollution, investigation of cases against corruption and electoral reforms that are ordinarily handled by the executive under the control of the legislature are being resolved by the judiciary. Judicial activism also violates the democratic principle of respecting the powers, and jurisdiction of each organ of the government, as it confers extraordinary powers on the judiciary.

Thus, the balance between the three organs of the government has become very delicate.

9. PIL is an important tool of Judicial Activism. Explain. **[NCERT]**

Ans. Judicial Activism or Public Interest Litigation have revolutionised the functioning of judiciary and made it more people friendly. The chief instrument through which judicial activism has flourished in India is PIL. Importance of PIL are as follows

- A person or a group can file a litigation in court on behalf of an individual of society in matters of public interest and not for personal cause.
- This has opened the gates for large number of cases where public spirited citizens and voluntary organisations sought judicial intervention for protection of existing rights, betterment of life conditions of poor, protection of the environment, and many other issues in the interest of public.
- Judiciary began considering cases merely on the basis of newspaper reports and postal complaints received by the court and the role of judiciary became more popular by judicial activism.

10. How is judicial activism related to the protection of Fundamental Rights? Has it helped in expanding the scope of Fundamental Rights? **[NCERT]**

Ans. Judicial activism is related to the protection of the Fundamental Rights as

- It has made the judiciary more approachable by the common people seeking justice.
- The Supreme Court has the power to remedy the violation of Fundamental Rights by issuing writs or by reviewing and declaring certain laws as unconstitutional.
- The PIL helps the poor to fight against discrimination.
- Inhumane working conditions, sexual exploitation of the children, blinding of jail inmates by the police are some of the cases that have been considered by the courts, which have made rights meaningful and useful for the poor and disadvantaged people.
- Issues related to better living conditions, like clean air and water and pollution free environment, have also helped in the expansion of the scope of Fundamental Rights.

Thus, by these ways, it helped in expanding the scope of Fundamental Rights.

11. What was the ruling of the famous case of Keshavananda Bharti?

Ans. It 1973, the Supreme Court gave a decision that has become very important in regulating the relations between the Parliament and Judiciary since then. This case is famous as the Kesvananda Bharti Case. It was very controversial and dealt with issue that was bone of contention between the judiciary and legislature. The Supreme Court ruled out following in this case

- The basic structure of the Constitution cannot be violated even by the Parliament.
- It declared, right to property is not part of the basic structure.
- The court reserved to itself the right to decide whether any matter is a part of the basic structure or not.
- This ruling has changed the nature of conflicts between the Legislature and Judiciary.

12. Give some suggestions to ensure fast and inexpensive justice in India.

Ans. The main suggestions to ensure speedy and inexpensive justice in India are as following

(i) In every state of India the 'Lok-Adalats' should be established and organised at the state as well as district levels and there should be made popular among the people through publicity.

(ii) The instruments of judicial activism should be availed which has expanded the idea of rights and duties.

(iii) The pendency of cases should be facilitated and decided as early as possible.

(iv) Fees of courts and advocates should be controlled upto minimum extent.

(v) Through PIL, the court has expanded the idea of rights, clean air, unpolluted water, decent living etc. The judiciary takes these rights into consideration for those people also who cannot approach easily to the courts. And hence the problems of the poor people are settled.

Thus, the speedy and inexpensive justice may be availed by the citizens.

• Long Answer Type Questions

1. Discuss the means to provide and protect the independence of judiciary. **[NCERT]**

Ans. The Constitution of India has ensured the independence of judiciary through various measures.

The measure are

- The legislature is not involved in the process of appointment of judges. Thus, party politics are not involved in the process of appointment.
- A person must have an experience as a lawyer or must be versed, in law, to be appointed as judge. Person's political opinions or political loyalty should not be the criteria for appointment to the 'judiciary'.

- In order to function without fear the Constitution of India has given a fixed tenure to the judges. The Constitution prescribes very difficult procedure for the removal of judges to provide security of office to the members of judiciary.
- The judiciary is not financially dependent on either the executive or legislature. The salaries and allowances of the judges are not subjected to the approval of the Parliament as prescribed by the Constitution.
- The actions and decisions of the judges are immune from personal criticism and the judiciary has the power to penalise those guilty of contempt of court.
- Parliament cannot discuss the conduct of judges except when the proceedings for removal is carried out.

2. "India has an integrated judiciary". What does this statement mean?

Ans. India's judicial system is pyramidal in nature. At the apex of country's judicial system is the Supreme Court which is supreme gardian of the law of the land, comprising of Chief Justice and 25 other judges.

There are High Courts at the state level which have jurisdiction over a state, or a union territories.

Then there are District Courts which are established by the state governments which have authority over district or a group of districts. We have subordinate courts in districts which are of civil and criminal in nature.

Gram Nayayalyas have also been established at Panchayat level from 2008.

In India, Supreme Court is the highest court of appeal, which hear cases that comes as an appeal from the High Courts. The Supreme Court's decisions are binding on all other courts of the country. Likewise, the Constitution has also defined the appellate jurisdiction of the High Courts as well which hear cases as an appeal from district courts and district courts hear cases that comes as an appeal from subordinate courts. This is why we say that India has an Integrated Judicial System.

3. Describe the various jurisdictions of Supreme Court.

Ans. The Jurisdictions of Supreme Court are as follows

- **Original Jurisdiction** It means when the cases are directly considered by the Supreme Court and it alone has the power to deal with such cases. Neither the High Court nor the lower courts have the power to deal with such cases. For instance, disputes between Union and States and amongst the states.
- **Writ Jurisdiction** When the Fundamental Rights of an individual is violated and the aggrieved person approach directly to the Supreme Court. It issues a special order like Habeas Corpus, Mandamus, Certiorari, Quo Warranto and Prohibition to be followed in the form of writs. This jurisdiction is known as 'writ jurisdiction'.
- **Appellate Jurisdiction** The Supreme Court is the highest court of appeal. Appellate jurisdiction means that Supreme Court will reconsider the decisions

made by the High Court in various matters and the lower courts involving death sentence or criminal matters. However, the High Court must certify the fitness of appeal and the Supreme Court holds the power to decide whether to admit appeal even when the appeal is not allowed by the High Court.

- **Advisory Jurisdiction** The Supreme Court of India possesses advisory jurisdiction which means that President of India can refer any matter of public importance or constitutional interpretation to Supreme Court is not bound to give advice and the President is not bound to accept such advice.

4. Discuss the functions of the judiciary in India.

Ans. The judiciary has following functions

- **It interprets the Laws** A lot of instances are presented before the judges in which the issue of law interpretation arises, because the law is not clear in such cases. Even cases where the laws are silent are brought before them. The judges make decisions in certain issues or matters. These rulings are later cited in comparable instances. In this approach, the courts inadvertently expand the law.
- **Protector of Civil Rights** The state grants people many rights through the Legislation of Parliament. These rights are safeguarded by the courts.
- **Decides the Cases** Many Cases involving issues between citizens or between the government and citizens are heard by the courts. In such cases, the courts make their judgements.
- **Custodian of Fundamental Rights** In today's world, many countries' constitutions offer citizens Fundamental Rights. These rights are guarded by the Supreme Courts in such countries. If a citizen violates these Fundamental Rights, or if a person loses his or her rights as a result of the violation, an appeal to a High Court or the Supreme Court can be made to safeguard those rights. The courts have a responsibility to preserve citizens' rights.
- **Power to get its Decisions and Judgements Enforced** The judiciary has the power not only to deliver judgements and decide disputes, but also to get these enforced. It can direct the executive to carry out its decisions. It can summon any person and directly know the truth from him.
- **In Federations, Resolves issues of Jurisdiction between the Centre and State governments** There is a separation of powers between the Central Government and the States in federal constitutions. The risk of a jurisdictional disagreement between the Centre and the State exists. As a result, the Supreme Court is given the authority to resolve these conflicts.
- **Advisory Functions** Very often the courts are given the responsibility to give advisory opinions to the rulers on any legal matter. For example, the President of India the power to refer to the Supreme Court any question of law or fact which is of public importance.

5. What are the impacts of judicial activism?

Ans. The impact of judicial activism is two-fold such as

Positive Impacts

- It has democratised the judicial system by giving not just to individuals but also the group access to courts.
- It has forced executive accountability.
- It has also made an attempt to make the electoral system much more free and fair, as the courts ask candidate contesting elections to file affidavit declaring the assets and income along with their educational qualifications so that the people could elect their representatives based on accurate knowledge.

Negative Impacts

- PIL has overburdened the courts.
- Judicial activism has blurred the line of distinction between the executive and legislature on one hand and the judiciary on the other.
- The court is involved in resolving the questions which belongs to executive such as, reducing air or sound pollution or investigating cases of corruption, or bringing about electoral reforms, which is not exactly the duty of judiciary
- Supreme Court for advice. However, the Supreme Court is not bound to give advice and the President is not bound to accept such advice.

• Case Based Questions

1. Read the passage and answer the questions that follow.

The appointment of judges has never been free from political controversy. It is part of the political process. It makes a difference who serves in the Supreme Court and High Court a difference in how the Constitution is interpreted. The political philosophy of the judges, their views about active and assertive judiciary or controlled and committed judiciary have an impact on the fate of the legislations enacted….a convention had developed whereby the senior-most judge of the Supreme Court was appointed as the Chief Justice of India….CJI superseding three senior Judges, Justice M.H. Beg was appointed superseding Justice H.R. Khanna (1975).

(i) Who was appointed as the Chief Justice of India in 1975?

(ii) What is the role of Executive and Legislature in the process of appointment of Judges?

(iii) What is the collegium system?

Ans. (i) The Chief Justice of India superseding three senior Judges during the time of Indira Gandhi and appointed M.H. Beg as the new CJI in 1975.

(ii) The judges are appointed by the President of India after the government ratified the name suggest by the collegium system. There is no role of legislature in appointing the judges.

(iii) The method of appointing and transferring judges has evolved as a result of Supreme Court decisions rather than an Act of Parliament or a provision of the Constitution and the government is only involved after the collegium has settled on names. The collegium system consists of the Chief Justice of India and the four senior most Judges of the Supreme Court.

2. Read the following source and answer the questions that follow.

There are many other instances in which the Supreme Court actively involved itself in the administration of justice by giving directions to executive agencies. The Indian Constitution is based on a delicate principle of limited separation of powers and checks and balances. This means that each organ of the government has a clear area of functioning. Thus, the Parliament is supreme in making laws and amending the Constitution, the executive is supreme in implementing them while the judiciary is supreme in settling disputes and deciding whether the laws that have been made are in accordance with the provisions of the Constitution.

(i) Which of the following system does India follows to keep an eye on the organs of the Government?

(ii) What is the separation of powers in the Constitution?

(iii) What is the role of different organs of the government?

Ans. (i) The Indian Constitution is based on a delicate principle of limited separation of powers and checks and balances.

(ii) The separation of power is based on the concept of trias politica. It reduces the possibility of arbitrary government actions by requiring the approval of all three branches when making, enforcing, and administering laws.

(iii) The Parliament is supreme in making laws and amending the Constitution, the executive is supreme in implementing them while the judiciary is supreme in settling disputes and deciding whether the laws that have been made are in accordance with the provisions of the Constitution.

3. Observe the cartoon given below and answer the questions that follow.

(i) Identify the values shown in the above picture?

(ii) Discuss the weakness of Indian judicial system?

(iii) How active is the judiciary in combating corruption is the public sector?

Ans. (i) The values shown in the above picture are independent judiciary, integration and protection of citizens.

(ii) The weaknesses of Indian judicial system are as follows

- Justice is very costly in India. It is difficult for a poor man to get justice from the court. Very high fee is demanded by the lawyers and there are various other expenses which a poor man cannot afford.

- The judicial system of India is very time consuming, where cases are running from 10 years, 15 years, etc.

- There are lack of judges in courts, seats are running vacant and files of cases are getting piled-up day-by-day.

(iii) The judiciary is a powerful institution that prides itself on its independence. Many people's rights have been preserved by diverse interpretations of the constitution. The Supreme Court frequently participates in the administration of justice by issuing directives to governmental authorities.

4. Observe the cartoon given below and answer the questions that follow.

(i) What is the cartoon about?

(ii) What message is being conveyed through the cartoon?

(iii) What are the instruments of Judicial Activism?

Ans. (i) This cartoon is about judicial activism.

(ii) The cartoon conveys that bandh and hartals are illegal, as many people think that these two things has revolutionised the functioning of judiciary and made it more people-friendly.

(iii) The instruments of judicial activism are Public Interest Litigation or Social Action Litigation and Judicial Review.

- **Objective Type Questions**

  1 The Judges of the High Court are appointed by the ....
  (a) Governor　　　　　　　　　　　　(b) President
  (c) Prime Minister　　　　　　　　　　(d) Chief Minister

  2 Who among the following is appointed by the President as the Chief Justice of India?
  (a) Seniormost Judge of Supreme Court　　(b) as recommended by Council of India
  (c) President of Bar Council of India　　　(d) Seniormost High Court Judge

  3 What is PIL?
  (a) Public Information Letter　　　　　　(b) People's Interest Litigation
  (c) Public Interest Litigation　　　　　　(d) People's Information Law

  4 .... majority is required in procedure of removal of Judges.
  (a) Simple　　　　　　　　　　　　　(b) Special
  (c) Effective　　　　　　　　　　　　(d) Absolute

  5 Who among the following has the power to issue writs for enforcement of Fundamental Rights?
  (a) Supreme Court　　　　　　　　　　(b) High Court
  (c) President　　　　　　　　　　　　(d) Both (a) and (b)

- **Short Answer Type Questions**

  1 State the composition of Supreme Court of India.
  2 Write a short note on Judicial Review.
  3 Judicial activism can lead to conflict between the executive and the judiciary. Justify.
  4 Comment on the relationship between the judiciary and Parliament.
  5 How can a judge of Supreme or High Court be removed from office?
  6 What has the constitution formulated to preserve the independence of the judiciary?
  7 What qualifications have been laid down for being appointed as a judge of the High Court?

- **Long Answer Type Questions**

  1 Supreme Court is the guarantor of Fundamental Rights. Explain.
  2 Discuss the functions of the judiciary in India.
  3 Explain in detail the power of Judicial Review of Supreme Court of India.
  4 Elucidate the jurisdictions of Supreme Court of India.

CHAPTER 01

Liberty

In this Chapter...
- Meaning of Liberty
- Meaning of Freedom
- Significance of Freedom
- Harm Principle of Freedom
- Meaning of Negative and Positive Liberty
- Freedom of Expression

Liberty is the quality of being free whereas, **freedom** signifies **absence of restrictions** and **constraints** on individual actions. The struggle for freedom represents the desire of people to be in control of their own lives and to have the opportunity to express themselves freely through their choices and activities.

Meaning of Liberty

The state of being free within society from authority's control or harsh constraints on one's way of life, behaviour or political opinions is known as liberty. As a result, liberty implies the responsible exercise of freedom under the rule of law without endangering the liberty of others. Because peace and order in society can only be maintained by imposing some limits on people, liberty does not imply the absence of all limits. Only a positive social context allows for the enjoyment of liberty.

Importance of Liberty

- It allows people to pursue their goals. Liberty is uncommon, valuable, never guaranteed and always at risk. If it is not advanced and defended, it can be lost in a single generation.
- To be completely human, we must all be free to make our own decisions and manage our own lives as long as we allow others to do the same.
- Liberty is effective. Nothing else even comes close to producing the level of interpersonal collaboration, invention and wealth creation that permits human beings to prosper.

Meaning of Freedom

Freedom is a political term which allows an individual to make choices and to exercise independent judgement. In other words, an individual could be considered free if he/she is not subject to external controls; if he/she is able to make independent decisions and act in an autonomous way. One aspect of freedom i.e. the **absence of external constraints** and the another important aspect is **existence of conditions** in which people can freely express themselves and develop their talents.

External constraints means the force or compulsions under which an individual has to work and absence of external constraints means that an individual should not be forced to perform any action which he/she does not want to perform.

A free society is one in which all of its members are able to reach their full potential with the least number of social restrictions. Freedom is admired because it encourages us to make our own decisions and use our judgement. It allows people to use their reasoning and decision-making abilities.

Liberty vs Freedom

Liberty and freedom are two different concepts. The fundamental difference between the two can be understand by their meaning.

Liberty comes from the Latin word *libertatem* which means condition of a freeman. While freedom come from the English word *freodom* which means state of free will.

Liberty is **power to act** and **express oneself** according to one's will while freedom is the **power to decide** one's action. Freedom is more concrete concept than liberty which is more associated with an individual's connection with the state rather than with other individuals and circumstances.

The difference between these two concepts can briefly be onlined as follows

Liberty	Freedom
Condition of a free man	State of free will
Power to act	Power to decide
Free to do something	Free from something

The common feature between these two concepts is that both remain unconstrained, which means that their realisation is **free from any constrain**. Futher, both follow rightful or ethical conformity in terms of their realisation.

Significance of Freedom

Freedom is significant due to the following reasons

- Freedom gives happiness because the state of being free is aligned with our true nature.
- It is the lifeline of civilised living, as without freedom we wouldn't be able to evolve.
- Freedom allows the full development of individual's creativity, sensibilities and capabilities like sports, science, art, music or exploration.
- Freedom is significant because it allows us to be ourselves while still allowing us to collaborate while retaining our independence.

Netaji Subhash Chandra Bose on Freedom

For Subhash Chandra Bose freedom means all round freedom i.e. freedom for the individual as well as for society; freedom for the rich as well as for the poor; freedom for men as well as for women; freedom for all individuals and for all classes. For him, freedom implies not only liberation from political bondage but also equal distribution of wealth, abolition of caste barriers and social inequities and destruction of Hind Swaraj communalism and religious intolerance.

Relation between Swaraj and Freedom

Swaraj means rule of self and rule over self. Swaraj was an important rallying cry in the freedom movement inspiring **Tilak** famous statements. "Swaraj is my birth right and I shall have it." It is the understanding of Swaraj as Rule over the self that was highlighted by **Mahatma Gandhi** in this work. It is not just freedom but liberation in redeeming one's self-respect, self-responsibility, and capacities for self-realisation from institution of dehumanisation.

Gandhiji believed the development that follows would liberate both individual and collective potentialities guided by the principle of Justice. It is as relevant to the 21st Century as it was when Gandhiji wrote the **Hind Swaraj** in 1909.

The Sources of Constraints (Restrictions) on Freedom

Individual independence can be restricted as a result of dominance and external controls. Such prohibitions can be imposed by force or by a government through laws that reflect the rulers' control over the people and which may have backing of force. This was the form of oppression imposed by colonial rulers on their subjects or by the system of apartheid regime in South Africa.

Some form of government is unavoidable. But democratic governments allow citizens to exercise some power over their rulers. As a result, democratic governance is regarded as an effective way of safeguarding people's rights.

Social injustice can also impose restrictions on democracy. For example, the kind implicit in the caste system, or the kind that results from a society's extreme economic inequality.

Need of Constraints on Freedom

Political and legal constraints are required or else society would descend into chaos. Differences may exist between people regarding their ideas and opinions, they may have conflicting ambitions, they may complete to control scarce resources. There are numerous reasons why disagreements may develop in a society which may express themselves through open conflict.

Therefore, every society needs some mechanisms to control violence and settle disputes. As long as we are able to respect each other's views and do not attempt to impose our views on others, we may be able to live freely and with minimum constraints. Some **legal** and **political** constraints are needed to ensure that differences may be discussed and debated without one group coercively (forcibly) imposing its views on the other.

The Ideals of Freedom

Nelson Mandela is considered as the greatest person of the 20th century to fight for freedom. He wrote a book **Long Walk to** Freedom in which he talks about his personal struggle against the apartheid regime (administration) in South Africa. For freedom of Black people in South Africa, Mandela spent 28 years of his life in jail, often in solitary confinement. After long struggle he became successful to get freedom.

Another person who fought for freedom is **Aung San Suu Kyi** who belongs to Myanmar. For her, Gandhi ji's thoughts on non-violence have been a sources of inspiration. She wrote a book titled Freedom from fear in which she said that real freedom is to live a dignified human life by over coming the fear.

Liberalism as a means of Tolerance

Liberalism identified has been **associated** with the importance of tolerance as a political philosophy. Liberals have always protected a express person's right to hold and **share** his or her own views and values, even though they disagree. However, libralism is more than just that. Tolerance is supported by many modern ideologies, not just liberalism.

Liberalism advocated for a free market economy with the government playing a minor role. Modern liberalism, on the other hand, recognises the position of the welfare state and the need for policies to address both social and economic inequality.

Harm Principle of Freedom

The harm principle of liberty was given by **John Stuart Mill** in his essay **On Liberty**. In this principle, Mill argues that the only justiciable reason to interfere with an individual's exercise of liberty is to prevent harm to others. Mill distinguishes between acts that are **self-regarding**, i.e. actions that only affect the particular actor and no one else, and actions that are **other-regarding**, i.e. actions that affect others as well.

He claims that with respect to action or choices that affect only one's self, self-regarding action, the state coramy other external authority has no business to interfere.

However, as freedom is at the core of human society and is so essential for living a dignified human life, it should only be limited in exceptional circumstances. The resulting 'damage' must be 'severe.' Mill advises only social disapproval rather than the force of law for minor injury.

The word **reasonable restrictions** is used in India's constitutional debates to describe such justifiable constraints. The restrictions which exist, but they must be fair, i.e. capable of being justified by reason, not excessive, and not out of proportion to the conduct being limited, since then it would jeopardise society's overall state of liberty. We must not cultivate the practise of enforcing limits, as this is harmful to liberty.

Meaning of Negative and Positive Liberty

In political theory, freedom as the absence of external constraints is called negative liberty while freedom as the expansion of opportunities to express one's self is called positive liberty.

Negative liberty seeks to define and defend an area in which the individual would be inviolable. This is an area in which no external authority can interfere. It is a minimum area in which the individual's actions are not to be interfered with.

The existence of the **minimum area of non-interference** is the recognition that human nature and dignity require an area where an individual can act freely without interference from others.

Positive liberty debates have a long history that can be traced back to thinkers like **Rousseau, Hegel, Marx, Gandhi and Aurobindo**, as well as those who draw inspiration from them. It is concerned with examining their circumstances and essence of the individual-society relationship in order to improve these conditions so that the growth of the individual personality is not hampered.

Positive liberty allows an individual to develop his or her capability with reasonable constraints. In this, an individual must not be constrained by poverty or unemployment, they must have adequate material resources to pursue their wants and needs.

Freedom of Expression

The freedom of expression is one of the issues that is regarded to fall under the minimum domain of **non-interference**. Freedom of expression is a fundamental value and for the society must be willing to put up with some inconvenience in order to safeguard it against those who would seek to limit it.

Deepa Mehta, a filmmaker, wanted to make a film about widows in Varanasi a few years ago. It attempted to investigate the condition of widows, but it was met with fierce opposition from a part of the population who believed it would portray India in a negative light, that it was being created to appeal to foreign audiences and that it would bring a bad name to the historic town.

They refused as a result it could not made in Varanasi similarly, some elements of society protested against Aubrey Menon's book **Ramayana Retold** and Salman Rushdie's **The Satanic Verses**. The film 'The Last Temptation of Christ' and the play **Me Nathuram Boltey** were also banned after protests.

As a result, various types of constraints exist and we are subject to them in various situations. When we consider such situations, we must remember that when restrictions are backed by organised societal - religious or cultural authority or the state's force, they restrict our freedom in ways that are difficult to fight again it.

However, if we willingly accept certain limits in order to pursue our goals or ambitions, our freedom is not similarly limited. In any event, we cannot claim that our freedom has been restricted if we are not forced to accept the conditions.

Freedom of expression is the freedom to communicate ideas without restraint, whether orally or in print or by any other means of communication. **John Stuart Mill**, a political thinker of the 19th century offered four reasons due to which there should be Freedom of Expression.

These are

- No idea is completely false. The idea which appears to us as false has an element of truth.
- Truth does not emerge by itself. It is only through a conflict of opposing views that emerges truth.
- Conflict of ideas is valuable not just in the past but is of continuing value for all times.
- We cannot be sure that the ideas we consider true is actually true.

Chapter Practice

Objective Questions

• Multiple Choice Questions

1. Consider the following statements related to importance of liberty?
   (a) If liberty is not defended, it can be lost in a multiple generation.
   (b) The goal of liberty is to allow people to pursue their passions.
   (c) Both (a) and (b)
   (d) None of the above

Ans. (b) The goal of liberty is to allow people to pursue their passions. Liberty is uncommon, valuable, never guaranteed and always at risk. If it is not advanced and defended, it can be lost in a single generation.

2. Consider the following statements:
   (a) Liberty has power to decide.
   (b) Freedom has power to act.
   (c) Liberty can only be positive
   (d) None of the above

Ans. (d) Liberty has power to act and freedom has power to decide and liberty can be negative and positive both. Hence (d) is the correct option.

3. Which of the following statements about freedom are incorrect?
   (a) Freedom is said to exist when external constraints on the individual are absent.
   (b) Freedom is also about expanding the ability of people to freely express themselves and develop their potential.
   (c) Freedom is the state of being able to express one's imagination and skill.
   (d) Absence of constraints is only dimension of freedom.

Ans. (d) All of these statements given about freedom are correct except option (d).

4. Which among the following is an important aspect of freedom in which people can develop their talents?
   (a) Absence of external constraints

   (b) Existence of inclusive conditions
   (c) Gender Neutral
   (d) Both (a) and (b)

Ans. (d) One aspect of freedom i.e., the absence of external constraints and another important aspect is existence of conditions in which people can freely express themselves and develop their talents.

5. Consider the following statement related to freedom.
   It has equal distribution of ....
   (i) Wealth
   (ii) Abolition of caste barriers and social inequities
   (iii) Destruction of communalism and religious intolerance
   Select the correct option.
   (a) Only (i)
   (b) Only (ii)
   (c) (ii) and (iii)
   (d) All of these

Ans. (d) For Subhash Chandra Bose freedom implies not only liberation from political bondage and social inequities and destruction of communalism and religious intolerance. Hence (d) is the correct option.

6. .... is not only equality, but also emancipation from structures that dehumanise one's self-respect, self-responsibility and capacities for self-realisation.
   (a) Constitution   (b) Liberty
   (c) Swaraj   (d) Rights

Ans. (c) Swaraj means rule of self and rule over self. It is not just freedom but liberation in redeeming one's self-respect, self-responsibility, and capacities for self-realisation from institution of dehumanisation.

7. The book , 'Long Walk to Freedom' was written by ....
   (a) Aung San Suu Kyi
   (b) Nelson Mandela
   (c) Subhash Chandra Bose
   (d) Bal Gangadhar Tilak

Ans. (b) A book 'Long Walk to Freedom' was written by Nelson Mandela.

8. Who among the following fought for the freedom of black people in South Africa?
   (a) Nelson Mandela   (b) Aung San Suu Kyi

(c) Thomas Jefferson　　　　(d) Rousseau

Ans. (a) Nelson Mandela has fought for the freedom of black people in South Africa.

9. For whom Gandhi's thoughts on non-violence have been a source of inspiration?
　(a) Aung San Suu Kyi　　　(b) Nelson Mandela
　(c) Subhash Chandra Bose　(d) Bal Gangadhar Tilak

Ans. (a) For Aung San Suu Kyi Gandhi's thought on non-violence have been the source of inspiration.

10. Who has given the concept of harm principle of liberty?
　(a) Nelson Mandela　　　　(b) John Stuart Mill
　(c) Thomas Jefferson　　　(d) Rousseau

Ans. (b) The harm principle of liberty was given by John Stuart Mill in his essay 'On Liberty'.

11. Who stood up for freedom of speech, including freedom of thinking and debate?
　(a) Nelson Mandela　　　　(b) John Stuart Mill
　(c) Thomas Jefferson　　　(d) Rousseau

Ans. (b) John Stuart Mill stood up for freedom of speech, including (a) freedom of thinking and debate.

12. Consider the following statements
　(i) The 'Harm Principle of Freedom' was given by Robert Nozick.
　(ii) According to John Mill, there are two kinds of action; Self-regarding and Other regarding.

　Which of the following statements/s is/are incorrect.
　(a) Only (i)　　　　　　　(b) Only (ii)
　(c) Both (i) and (ii)　　　(d) None of these

Ans. (a) The 'Harm Principle of Freedom' was given by John Stuart Mill in his essay 'On Liberty'.

13. The form of freedom in which the 'absence of external constraints' is most valuable is called
　............... .
　(a) Communitarian Liberty
　(b) Positive Liberty
　(c) Utilitarian Liberty
　(d) Negative Liberty

Ans. (d) The form of freedom in which the absence of external constraints is most valuable is called Negative liberty.

14. In the context of Indian Constitution, the term used for justifiable constraints is ....
　(a) Valid restrictions　　　(b) Justifiable restrictions
　(c) True restrictions　　　(d) Reasonable restrictions

Ans. (d) The word 'reasonable restrictions' is used in India's constitutional debates to describe such justifiable constraints.

15. It is concerned with examining the circumstances and essence of the individual-society relationship in order to improve the conditions.

The above statement is related to?
　(a) Negative Liberty　　　(b) Freedom
　(c) Positive Liberty　　　(d) Communitarian Liberty

Ans. (c) Positive Liberty

• Assertion-Reasoning MCQs

Directions (Q. Nos. 16-20) In the questions given below, there are two statements marked as Assertion (A) and Reason (R). Read the statements and choose the correct option.

　Codes
　(a) Both A and R are true and R is the correct explanation of A.
　(b) Both A and R are true, but R is the not correct explanation of A.
　(c) A is true, but R is false.
　(d) A is false, but R is true.

16. **Assertion** (A) Liberty can be lost in a single generation.

Reason (R) Liberty is power to act and express oneself according to one's will while freedom is the power to decide one's action.

Ans. (b) Both the statements are correct and R is not the correct explanation of A because Assertion is about the importance of liberty while Reason is about the definition of liberty.

17. **Assertion** (A) Freedom of speech is the most important civil liberty of people in a democratic polity.

Reason (R) State can regulate free speech in the interest of public order.

Ans. (a) Both A and R are correct and R is the correct explanation of A.

18. **Assertion** (A) Liberty is more concrete concept than freedom.

Reason (R) More associated with an individual's connection with the state rather than with other individuals and circumstances.

Ans. (c) A is incorrect whereas R is correct. Freedom is more concrete concept than liberty.

19. **Assertion** (A) In India everyone has given some freedom rights under the constitution but subjected to reasonable restriction.

Reason (R) Reasonable restriction is necessary in order to protect Security of the State; Friendly Relation with Foreign States; Public Order; etc.

Ans. (a) Both the statements are correct and R is the correct explanation of A.

20. **Assertion** (A) Freedom of expression is the freedom to communicate ideas without restraint, whether orally or in print or by any other means of communication.

Reason (R) 'Negative liberty' allows an individual to develop his or her capability with reasonable constraints.

Ans. (d) A is correct and R is incorrect. 'Positive liberty' allows an individual to develop his or her capability with reasonable constraints.

• Case Based MCQs

1. Read the passage and answer the questions that follow.

Freedom is at the core of human society, is so crucial for a dignified human life, it should only be constrained in special circumstances. The harm caused must be 'serious. For minor harm, Mill recommends only social disapproval and not the force of law. For example, the playing of loud music in an apartment building should bring only social disapproval from the other residents of the building. They should not involve the police. They should indicate their disapproval, of the inconvenience that playing loud music has caused them, by perhaps refusing to greet the person who plays the music disregarding the harm it is causing others.

(i) Since .... is at the heart of human society and is so essential for living a meaningful life, it should only be restricted in extraordinary cases.
(a) liberty　　　　　　(b) freedom
(c) justice　　　　　　(d) equality

Ans. (b) Freedom is at the core of human society, is so crucial for a dignified human life, it should only be constrained in special circumstances.

(ii) .... advocated for a free market economy with the government playing a minor role.
(a) Regionalism　　　(b) Globalisation
(c) Liberalism　　　　(d) Privatisation

Ans. (c) Liberalism advocated for a free market economy with the government playing a minor role.

(iii) What has been recommended by JS Mill in case of minor harm?
(a) Minimum constraints
(b) Social approval
(c) Social disapproval
(d) Maximum constraints

Ans. (c) Mill recommends only social disapproval and not the force of law in case of minor harm.

(iv) .... is recognised as an essential way of safeguarding people's rights.
(a) Monarchical government
(b) Democratic government
(c) Republican government
(d) None of the above

Ans. (b) Democratic government.

(v) Consider the following statements.
1. Mill advises only force of law rather than the social disapproval for minor injury.
2. John Stuart distinguishes between acts that are 'self-regarding' and 'other-regarding,'.

Which of the statements given above is / are correct?
(a) Only 1　　　　　　(b) Only 2
(c) Both 1 and 2　　　(d) None of these

Ans. (d) Mill advises only social disapproval rather than the force of law for minor injury. Hence statement 1 is incorrect.
Mill distinguishes between acts that are 'self-regarding,' (action that affect individuals) and 'other-regarding,' that is, actions that affect others as well. Hence statement 2 is correct. Therefore (d) is the correct option.

PART 2
Subjective Questions

• Short Answer Type Questions

1. What are the importance of liberty?

Ans. The importance of liberty are as follows
- The goal of liberty is to allow people to pursue their passions. Liberty is uncommon, valuable, never guaranteed and always at risk. If it is not advanced and defended, it can be lost in a single generation.
- To be completely human, we must all be free to make our own decisions and manage our own lives as long as we allow others to do the same.
- Liberty is effective. Nothing else even comes close to producing the level of interpersonal collaboration, invention and wealth creation that permits human beings to prosper.

2. What are the differences between liberty and freedom?

Ans. Liberty and freedom are two different concepts. The fundamental difference between the two can be understand by their meaning.
- Liberty comes from the Latin word 'libertatem' which means 'condition of a freeman.' While freedom come from the English word 'freedom' which means 'state of free will'.
- Liberty is power to act and express oneself according to one's will while freedom is the power to decide one's action.
- Freedom is more concrete concept than liberty which is more associated with an individual's connection with the state rather than with other individuals and circumstances.

- Both follow rightful or ethical conformity in term of their realisation.

3. What is meant by freedom? Is there a relationship between freedom for the individual and freedom for the nation? **[NCERT]**

Ans. Freedom is a political term which allows an individual to make choices and to exercise independent judgement. Absolute freedom is not good for society. There should be reasonable constraints on freedom to maintain peace and harmony in society.

There is a close relationship between the freedom for the individual and freedom for the nation, which are as follows

- In a free nation, every citizen is given freedom to develop his potentials with minimum social constraints.
- Freedom is crucial for overall development of a nation as well as of an individual. If a nation is free from any external influence, it can take better decisions for development of that nation and its citizens.
- A free nation gives opportunities to its citizens to enhance creativities and capabilities.

4. Why the freedom is significant?

Ans. Freedom is significant due to the following reasons

- Freedom gives happiness because the state of being free is aligned with our true nature.
- It is the lifeline of civilised living, as without freedom we wouldn't be able to evolve.
- Freedom allows the full development of individual's creativity, sensibilities and capabilities like sports, science, art, music or exploration.
- Freedom is significant because it allows us to be ourselves while still allowing us to collaborate while retaining our independence.
- Freedom empowers man and provides him with the ability to freely express himself and develop his potential.

5. "Liberty implies reasonable restraints rather than absence of constraints." Write your views on this statement.

Ans. Liberty implies reasonable restraints rather than absence of constraints, so that we can respect the difference of ideas, beliefs and opinions in society. This will lead to maintenance of order and peace in society. John Stuart Mill says that freedom can be restrained only for self-protection which means if somebody's freedom harm the other person then that person's freedom can be restricted. Since freedom is very important for human life, so it should be constrained only in special circumstances, especially when harm is serious.

6. What is meant by social constraints? Are constraints of any kind necessary for enjoying freedom?

Ans. The domination and external controls on freedom of individual imposed by the society is known as social constraints. These controls may be imposed by the government through laws or constitution which embody the power of the rulers over the people. Constraints of different kind exist and we are subject to them in different situations. Constraints on freedom can also result from social inequality of the kind implicit in the caste system, or result from extreme economic inequality in a society.

Yes, the constraints are necessary for enjoying freedom because

- It is essential for the creation of a peaceful society.
- It develops respect for differences of views, opinions and beliefs.
- It is required to control violence and settle disputes.

7. What are the views of Subhash Chandra Bose on freedom?

Ans. For Subhash Chandra Bose freedom means all round freedom i.e. freedom for the individual as well as for society; freedom for the rich as well as for the poor; freedom for men as well as for women; freedom for all individuals and for all classes. In short, his idea of freedom can be summed up as indusive growth.

For him, freedom implies not only liberation from political bondage but also equal distribution of wealth, abolition of caste barriers and social inequities and destruction of communalism and religious intolerance.

8. What is Swaraj? Explain in detail.

Ans. Swaraj means self and raj means rule. It means rule of self and rule over self. Rule of self refers to freedom from British rule and attainment of freedom for India and rule over self means not just political freedom but also economic, social cultural freedom. Economic freedom means removal of poverty and having employment.

Social freedom means where people from different castes and religion are not discriminated and everybody is treated equally. Cultural freedom where all religions and cultures are equally respected. This type of freedom will help in gaining self-respect and dignity for everybody.

9. What is harm principle of JS Mill?

Ans. John Stuart Mill says that there are two kinds of actions i.e. self-regarding actions and other-regarding actions. Self-regarding actions are those actions which affect the individual only, and other regarding actions are those actions which affect the society.

Harm principle signifies that there should be justiciable reason for imposing restrictions on individuals exercise of liberty to prevent it from harming others. Mill says that 'Harm' is something that would injure the rights of someone else or set back important interests that benefit others.

10. What do you mean by negative liberty?

Ans. 'Negative liberty' seeks to define and defend and area in which the individual would be inviolable. It is the absence of obstacles, barriers or constraints. Negative liberty explains the idea 'freedom from' which means freedom from state, family, community, authority, etc. An area where no authority can interfere is negative liberty.

It is the minimum area that is sacred and in which whatever the individual does is not to be interfered with. In negative liberty, an individual can do whatever he/she wants to do. Political thinkers believe that state should not interfere in the choices of an individual, e.g. choices of dress, living, food, travelling, etc.

11. In what ways a state can safeguard the freedom of its citizens?

Ans. A state can safeguard the freedom of its citizens in following ways

- By giving Fundamental Rights for the basic and essential conditions of good life for their progress.
- By giving responsibilities to its citizens to maintain peace and harmony in society.
- By establishing equality before law.
- By giving privilege to minority groups.
- States maintain reasonable restrictions on its citizen so that they cannot harm the rights of other.
- The government is controlled by the state. So whatever the government does it affect the freedom of citizens.

12. "Freedom is valuable for human progress". Write your views on this statement.

Ans. Freedom is necessary to generate progress. People also value freedom as an important component of progress. With freedom, individuals become liberated from the past constraints of aristocratic and social bondage. They will become more independent, happy and self-determining. Over the last 200 years, mankind has made remarkable progress in extending personal freedoms.

Today, one-third of the world enjoys freedom. In the years following the Second World War, political freedom has grown significantly throughout the world. Without freedom, there will be little or no progress in individual or society as well. Freedom is correlated, not only with democracy, but with human satisfaction also.

13. "No individual living in society can hope to enjoy total absence of any kind of constraints or restrictions." Explain the practicability of this statement in your life.

Ans. French scholar Voltaire disapproves any kind of constraint for full enjoyment of freedom. He was committed to unrestricted freedom of expression. The practicability of this statement can be seen as following

- On the name of liberty and freedom of expression, a number of people manipulate the situations.
- To handle social problems like child abuse, dowry, separation, divorce, alcoholism, etc, reasonable restrictions or constraints are essential for freedom.
- Man is a social animal and in an ideal society no one can hope for absolute enjoyment of freedom.

- If there would no restrictions or constraints on individual liberty, there would be social disharmony and man will behave as an animal.

14. "Democratic government is considered to be an important means of protecting the freedom of people." Justify this statement.

Ans. Democratic Government is considered to be an important means of protecting the freedom of people due to following reasons

- In democratic government, power and civic responsibility are exercised by all citizens, directly or through their freely elected representatives.
- Democratic government is a set of principles and practices that protect human freedom.
- Citizens in a democratic government have not only rights but they also have the responsibility to participate in the political system that in turn protects their rights and freedom.

15. Do you think that freedom of expression is essential to protect the interests of every individual in society? Give examples to support your answer.

Ans. Freedom of expression is essential to protect the interests of every individual in society because it laid the foundation of a democratic society. Freedom of expression is a very significant freedom which gives us opportunity to participate in democratic processes. Free, independent and diverse idea are essential for democracy. For example, ideas are expressed by films, books, movies, plays, paintings and social networking sites.

Sometimes films, books, movies, paintings are banned. Banning should be there, but it should not be politically motivated. There should be strong rationale behind it. Banning should not be regularly, otherwise state gets into habit of banning every time. While enjoying this freedom, people should take care that there should not be hatred campaigns and hatred speeches against anyone.

• Long Answer Type Questions

1. What is liberalism? How is liberalism associated with freedom?

Ans. Liberalism is a political ideology which forwards the idea that individuals are naturally endowed with reason and as such be allowed to enjoy the maximum possible freedom.

Liberalism is associated with freedom in the following ways

- It emphasises on individual's choices and interests. Only individuals are valuable for their choices, e.g., in terms of marriage, only the individuals have full freedom to choose his/ her life partner.
- Parents or community play only formal role. Liberals give priority to individual's liberty rather than equality.
- Minimum Administrative Control or Freedom Classical liberalism used to focus on minimal state control where state has only few roles to play as maintaining law and order.

- Now, liberal state calls for welfare state where the individual is allowed to pursue its own activities but at the same time state take measures to reduce social and economic inequalities.

2. "No idea is completely false. What appears to us as false has an element of truth." Justify this statement in context of freedom.

Ans. "No idea is completely false. What appears to us as false has an element of truth." This statement can be justified in following ways

- JS Mill says that no idea in this world is false. For example, if your parents tell you to become a doctor, engineer or lawyer, etc they are not wrong because they know that it will brighten your future prospects. But if you do not want to go for such career options, then you are also not wrong because you are having interest in some other areas and you think you can brighten your future prospects there. So, nobody is false and nobody is at fault.

- Truth does not emerge by itself. It is only through debates and discussion that truth emerges. Discussion between parents and a young child can lead to the conclusion that the child will go for higher studies. In this way, a child will be able to follow his passion in his area of interest and he will also follow his parents dream of going for higher studies.

- We cannot be sure that the ideas which we considered true is actually true. Ideas which were true at one point of time are false at another point of time. The society that completely suppresses the idea is not acceptable today, and it runs the danger of losing very valuable knowledge.

3. What are different kinds of liberty? Explain with examples.

Ans. Different kinds of freedom/liberty are as follows

- **Natural Liberty** It refers to unrestrained freedom to do whatever one likes. It means man is to be free from any superior power on earth, and not to be under the will or legislative authority of another man, but only to have the law of nature for his rule. For example, every person has freedom to live his life in his own way.

- **Civil Liberty** Civil liberty indicates that absence of such restraints which are not reasonable and legitimate. It denotes the enjoyment of our rights within the limits of law. For example, if an individual wants to listen music of his/her choice, he/she has full freedom to do so but its volume should not cross the limit set by the law.

- **Political Liberty** This is the freedom of citizens to participate in the political life and affairs of the state. The Right to Vote, the Right to Contest Elections, the Right to Hold Public Office, the Right to Express Political Views and the Right to Criticise the Government, etc. are examples of political liberty.

- **Economic Liberty** It refers to freedom of an individual to earn livelihood for survival. For example, every individual, regardless of the distinction of caste, colour and creed, should have liberty to earn his daily needs by fair means.

- **Personal/Individual Liberty** It means the availability of those conditions in which the individual can act as the person without being under any type of arbitrary and illegitimate restraint. For example, every individual should have the liberty to choose dress, food, standard of living, marriage, education of children, etc.

4. What is the difference between the negative and positive conception of liberty? **[NCERT]**

Ans. Following are differences between negative liberty and positive liberty.

Ans. Negative Conception of Liberty

- It is only concerned with the inviolable area in which no external authority can interfere.

- It implies the absence of restraints and rights to do whatever one likes.

- This conception may make the powerful person more powerful to keep the weaker ones on their mercy. This conception of liberty faces the following drawbacks:

- Liberty is concerned with the area control, not with its source, hence, this is not necessary to have democracy to enjoy freedom.

- The state should control the liberty of an individual only up to the limit where he interferes in other's such liberty.

Positive Conception of Liberty

- It recognises that an individual is free in society only and hence tries to make such societies which enables the development of the individual.

- It refers to the society in which adequate facilities are available for each and every section of society to enjoy desirable rights.

- This believes that any individual or section should not hinder the progress of others.

- People can enjoy all freedoms which are permissible by laws.

- It ensures the growth of poor, weak and downtrodden people also.

- It interprets that liberty lies in the removal of hindrances.

5. What is modern liberalism? What is the role of the state in upholding freedom of its citizens?

Ans. Liberalism has been identified with tolerance. It means the right of person to hold and express his/her opinions and beliefs should be defended. Modern liberalism focuses on individual. It emphasises on individual's choices and interests. Modern liberals give priority to individual liberty rather than equality. For example, in terms of marriage, only the individuals will be heard, not their parents or community.

The role of the state in upholding freedom of its citizens is

- The state provides certain rights to its citizens.

- The state maintains reasonable restrictions on its citizens so that they cannot harm the rights of others.

- The state provides positive liberty to its citizens so that they can expand their ability and talent.

- The state puts reasonable restrictions on freedom of its citizens in order to maintain social stability.

- A welfare state is always woried to protect the freedom of downtrodden people, of backward castes, economically and educationally weaker section and senior citizen as well as women.
- A state is controlled by the government because, whatever the government does, it affect, the freedom of citizens and if any conflict becomes violent, it hinders day-to-day life of state.

• Case Based Questions

1. Read the passage and answer the questions that follow.

Individual independence can be restricted as a result of dominance and external controls. Such prohibitions can be imposed by compulsion or by a government through laws that reflect the rulers' control over the people and can be enforced with force. This was the form of oppression imposed by colonial rulers on their subjects, or the apartheid regime in South Africa. Some form of government is unavoidable, democratic governments allow citizens to exercise some power over their rulers. As a result, democratic governance is regarded as an effective way of safeguarding people's rights. Social injustice can also impose restrictions on democracy. For example, the kind implicit in the caste system, or the kind that results from a society's extreme economic inequality.

(i) How individual independence can be restricted?

(ii) Who fought for the black people in South Africa?

(iii) Which forms of governance is important to safeguard people's rights?

Ans. (i) Individual independence can be restricted as a result of dominance and external controls. Such prohibitions can be imposed by compulsion or by a government through laws that reflect the rulers' control over the people and can be enforced with force.

(ii) For the freedom of Black people in South Africa, Nelson Mandela spent 28 years of his life in jail.

(iii) Democratic governance is regarded as an effective way of safeguarding people's rights.

2. Read the passage and answer the questions that follow.

The existence of the 'minimum area of non-interference' is a recognition that human nature and dignity require an area where an individual can act freely without interference from others. It is concerned with examining the circumstances and essence of the individual-society relationship in order to improve these conditions so that the growth of the individual personality is not hampered. 'Positive liberty' allows an individual to develop his or her capability with reasonable constraints. Individual must not be constrained by poverty or unemployment; they must have adequate material resources to pursue their wants and needs.

(i) What are the two aspects of Liberty?

(ii) What is the minimum area of non-interference?

(iii) On what terms, individuals must not be constrained?

Ans. (i) Positive and Negative are the two aspects of liberty.

(ii) The existence of the 'minimum area of non-interference' is a recognition that human nature and dignity require an area where an individual can act freely without interference from others.

(iii) Individual must not be constrained by poverty or unemployment; they must have adequate material resources to pursue their wants and needs.

Chapter Test

- **Objective Choice Questions**

  1 In the context of Indian constitution, the term used for justifiable constraints is ....

     (a) Valid restrictions
     (b) Justifiable restrictions
     (c) True restrictions
     (d) Reasonable restrictions

  2 Who wrote the Book 'Hind Swaraj'?

     (a) BG Tilak
     (b) MK Gandhi
     (c) JL Nehru
     (d) SC Bose

  3 Who divided actions into 'other regarding' & 'self regarding'?

     (a) John Locke
     (b) Nelson Mandela
     (c) John Mill
     (d) Aubrey Menon

  4 .... is the quality of being free whereas .... signifies absence of restrictions and constraints.

     (a) Freedom, equality
     (b) Equality, justice
     (c) Freedom, liberty
     (d) Liberty, freedom

  5 Liber means ....

     (a) no freedom
     (b) free
     (c) dimited freedom
     (d) None of these

  6 .... as an ideology, favours protection of individual rights, free market and minimal role of the state.

     (a) Communism
     (b) Republicanism
     (c) Liberalism
     (d) Utilitarianism

- **Short Answer Type Questions**

  1 Why the value of 'tolerance' is emphasised in liberalism?

  2 What has changed in classical and modern liberalism? Illustrate with examples.

  3 Why law is considered as an essential condition of liberty?

  4 What are the influences of liberalism on the Indian Constitution?

  5 What are the necessities of constraints to enjoy liberty?

  6 Two kinds of actions are given by JS Mill. Does Mill call for law to interfere in all kinds of 'other regarding actions'?

  7 Differentiate between classical and modern liberalism.

- **Long Answer Type Questions**

  1 Discuss the relationship between liberty and authority.

  2 Discuss political, economic and moral liberty.

  3 What are the reasons given by JS Mill for protecting freedom of speech and expression?

Equality

In this Chapter...

- Meaning of Equality
- Significance of Equality
- Three Dimensions of Equality
- Measures to Promote Equality

Meaning of Equality

Equality is a powerful moral and political ideal which aims to ensure that everyone gets the same status and rights in order to enjoy his life.

The inequalities in people's access to **basic requirements** like education healthcare, safe housing make an unequal and unjust society. Equality can be achieved by making sure that everyone is supported to have access to resources and decision making and he is to be recognised, valued and respected.

We consider it unfair when people are treated differently simply because they were born into a specific faith, ethnicity, caste, or gender. Humans, on the other hand, will have varying aspirations and objectives, and not all will be good.

Some people become great musicians, while others are known for their hard work and conscientiousness. The pursuit of the principle of equality does not mean the abolition of all differences. It simply implies that our care and prospects should not be predetermined by our birth or social circumstances.

Significance of Equality

- The concept of equality, as a **political ideal**, implies that all human beings are of equal value, regardless of their colour, gender, ethnicity, or nationality, because of their shared nature.
- It maintains that all humans deserve equal consideration and respect.
- It is this idea of a common society that underpins concepts like **universal human rights** and **crimes against humanity**.

The equality of all human beings has been rallying point in modern day movements against states and social institutions that maintain inequalities of rank, wealth position or privilege among people.

The French revolutionaries used the slogan **Liberty, Equality** and **Fraternity** to protest against the monarchy and the landed feudal aristocracy in the eighteenth century.

During anti-colonial independence movements in Asia and Africa in the twentieth century, the demand for equality was also increased. Women and Dalits, for example, who feel marginalised in our society, continue to raise the issue. Today, equality is a widely accepted ideal which is enshrined in many countries' constitutions and laws of many countries.

Equality of Opportunities

This concept implies that all human beings are entitled to the same rights and opportunities to develop their skills and talents, and to pursue their goals and ambitions. This means that people in a society can have different choices and desires. They can also have various strengths and abilities, resulting in some becoming more successful than others in their chosen professions.

In other words, it is the inequalities in people's access to such basic goods as education, health care and healthy housing that make for an unequal and unjust society, not the lack of equality of status, income or privilege.

Natural and Social Inequalities

Natural inequalities are those that emerge between people as a result of their different capabilities and talents. Natural inequalities are considered to be the result of the different characteristics and abilities with which people are born. It is assumed that natural inequalities cannot be altered.

They may treat people of different races, colours, genders and castes differently. Differences of this nature reflect a society's ideals, and some of them may appear to us to be unjust.

Social inequalities are created by society. Certain communities, for example, may favour and honour individuals who conduct intellectual work over those who conduct manual work. Discrimination on the basis of gender, caste, region and religion, etc. are inequalities created by society.

For example, women were for long described as **the weaker sex**, timid and of lesser intelligence than men and need special protection. Therfore, it was felt that denying women equal rights could be justified.

Differences of this nature represent a society's values, and some of these can seem to us to be unfair. This distinction can be helpful in distinguishing between legitimate and unequal differences in society, but it is not always straightforward or obvious. For example, because such inequalities in people's care have persisted for a long time, they can seem justified to us because they are based on inherent inequalities or traits that people are born with and cannot easily alter.

Another issue with the concept of natural differences is that certain differences that were once considered natural are no longer be seen be seen as unalterable. For example, advances medical science and technologies have made it possible for many disabled people to participate fully in society.

Three Dimensions of Equality

Based on different kinds of inequalities which exist in society, various thinkers and ideologies have highlight three main dimensions of equality i.e. Political, Social and Economic.

Political Equality

It includes granting equal citizenship to all the members of the state. The rights which are considered necessary to enable citizen to develop themselves and participate in the affairs of the state are right to vote, freedom of expressions, movement and association and freedom of belief. These rights are also considered as legal rights, which are guaranteed by constitution and laws.

Even in countries where all people have equal rights, significant inequalities will occur. Inequalities in the social and economic worlds are often the product of disparities in the wealth and opportunities available to people. As a result, demands for **fair rights** or a **level playing field**[1] are often

made. However, we must note that, although political and legal equality will not be sufficient to create a just and equitable society, it is unquestionably a necessary component.

Social Equality

Making equal laws are not sufficient, as we require equality in the access of resources (social goods). The pursuit of equality requires that people belonging to different groups and communities also have a fair and equal chance to compete for resources and opportunities. So, there is a need for equal, social and economic conditions like adequate provision of health care, education, nutrition and minimum wages. Unequal opportunities do not arise only from lack of goods but also from customs.

For example, women are not given equal rights in inheritance by some groups and also they are denied the opportunity of higher education in India. Thus, we need to make policies to prevent **discrimination** and **harassment** of women in public places or employment. The state has a significant role in such matters. But social groups and individual also have a role to play in raising awareness and supporting those who wants to exercise their rights.

Feminism

A political doctrine which advocates equal rights for women and men is called feminism. Feminists believe that social inequalities can be altered to live a free and equal lives. Feminism argue that inequality between men and women in society is the result of patriarchy. **Patriarchy** (Male dominated society) is based on the assumption that men and women are different by nature and this difference justifies their unequal position in society.

Feminists challenge this way of thinking by distinguishing between 'sex', which refers to the biological differences between men and women and 'gender' which determines the various roles that men and women perform in the society.

The biological reality that only women are capable of becoming pregnant and bearing children, which does not imply that only women should care for children once they are born. Feminists demonstrate that society, not nature, is responsible for much of the disparity between men and women.

Patriarchy creates a division of labour by which women are meant to be in charge of **private** and **domestic** concerns, while males are in charge of **public** tasks. Feminists call this difference into doubt, pointing out that most women are also involved in the 'Public' area.

That is, though the majority of women around the world work outside the home, they continue to be entirely responsible for household chores. Despite this **double burden** as feminists refer to it, women have little or no input decisions made in the public sphere. Feminism demand that discrimination between men and women, and all forms of gender inequalities should be eliminated.

---

1. **Level Playing Field** A situation in which everyone has a fair and equal chance of succeeding.

Economic Equality

When there is no significant differences in wealth, income and property between individuals or classes, then it leads to economic equality. The relative disparity between the wealthiest and poorest classes is one way to quantify the degree of economic inequality in a society. Another method will be to measure the number of people who live below the poverty line.

Entrenched inequalities or those that have remained largely unchanged over centuries, are more detrimental to a community. If certain groups of citizens in a society have accumulated significant wealth and the power that comes with it over centuries, the society will become divided between those classes and those who have remained poor over generations.

Views of Karl Marx on Equality

Karl Marx, a 19th century thinker says that entrenched inequality has come because of the **private ownership** and control of important economic resources like oil, land, forests and other forms of property. By owning such a great economic power, rich class also become politically powerful.

They influence state policies and laws which only safeguard the interest of wealthy class and are disadvantageous to the poor class. So, only by providing equal opportunities will not help the poor class, the need is to have state or public control over the resources and property of the society.

Views of Liberals on Equality

The thinkers of liberalism do not believe that political, economic and social inequalities are necessarily linked. They uphold the **principle of competition** as the most efficient and fair way of distributing resources and rewards in society.

The theory of competition, according to liberals, is the most just and effective way of choosing applicants for employment or admission to educational institutions. For example, in our country, many students aspire to enroll in professional programs and enrollment is extremely competitive. The government and courts have stepped in on occasion to control educational institutions and entrance exams in order to ensure that everybody has a fair and equitable opportunity to compete. Some people might indeed be turned away, but it is thought to be a reasonable way of distributing restricted seats.

The paradox (inconsistency) of equality accounts for the fact that ideal of equality is acceptable, but in reality we encounter inequality everywhere. In this complex world, everyone talks about equality but unequal wealth, opportunities, resources, work situations and power are visible everywhere. It raises many questions on ideal of equality and policy making.

<table>
<tr><td>

Socialism

Socialism is a set of political ideas which emerged as a response to the inequalities present in society that was produced by industrial **capitalist economy**. The basic objective of socialism is to minimise existing inequality in society and distribute resources justly.

Eminent socialist thinker **Rammanohar Lohia** identified seven kinds of inequalites. These are

1. Inequality between man and woman,
2. Inequality based on skin colour,
3. Caste-based inequality,
4. Colonial rule over some countries
5. Economic inequality
6. Revolution for civil liberties against unjust encroachments on private life
7. Revolution for Non-violence

For which struggle against inequality means struggle against these inequalities.

These were the seven revolutions or **Sapta Kranti** which was the **ideas of socialism** for Lohia.

</td></tr>
</table>

Measures to Promote Equality

Equality can be promoted through the following measures

Establishing Formal Equality

Social, economic and political inequalities all over the world have been protected by customs and legal system that prohibited some sections of society from enjoying certain kinds of opportunities and rewards.

The caste system in India prevented people from the 'lower' castes from doing anything except manual labour. To attain equality, all such restrictions or privileges should be brought to an end. The constitutions of most of the democratic government around the world have incorporated to prohibit discrimination on grounds of caste, race, sex, birth or religion. Our constitution also **abolishes** the practice of **untouchability** under **Article 17**.

The idea of equality has been publically adopted by most modern constitutions and democratic governments and it has been put into law as equal treatment for all citizens regardless of caste, race, religion or gender.

Equality through Differential Treatment

In special circumstances, it is necessary to treat different people differently in order to ensure that they can enjoy equal rights. For example, physically disabled people may justifiably demand special arrangement, so that they can get an equal chance to access facilities and resources.

It should not be seen as infringements of equality but as enhancement of equality. **Affirmative action** [2] programs have been used in several nations to improve equality of opportunity. In our country, we have relied on a **reservation policy**.

---

2. **Affirmative action** The practice or policy of favouring individuals belonging to groups known to have been discriminated against previously.

Affirmative Action

Affirmative actions are those actions which have an objective to take positive measures to minimise and eliminate social inequalities. In India, certain social groups or communities have been victims of social prejudice and discrimination in the form of exclusion and segregation (division).

Affirmative actions have been taken to provide them equality and justice. Such **socially backward communities** in India have been given reservation. Critics of positive discrimination says that reservation has led to reverse discrimination. It has denied other sections of society their right to equal treatment.

As a result, use the equality principle to reason against certain policies. They argue that the provision of reservations or quotas for the poor in admissions to higher education or employment is unjust because it denies other parts of society their right to equal care arbitrarily.

They argue that reservations are a form of reverse discrimination, and they continue to engage in activities that the equality principle challenges and opposes. Equality demands that all people are treated equally and making distinctions between people based on their caste or colour is likely to perpetuate caste and racial prejudices. Equality says that all people should be treated alike and we need to remove caste system to bring equality.

When considering the problem of equality its important to distinguish between treating everyone the same and trating everyone as equal. The latter may require special consideration on occasion, but in all circumstances, the fundamental goal is to promote equality.

Differential or special treatment may be considered in order to achieve equality but it must be justified and carefully evaluated.

Since the caste system and practices like apartheid included uneven treatment for different populations, liberals are normally sceptical of violations from the principle of equal treatment. The women's movement has addressed many of these questions related to the pursuit of equality. Women fought for fair rights in the nineteenth century. They demanded the same rights as men in their culture, such as the right to vote, the right to obtain degrees from colleges and universities and the right to work. However, when they joined the workforce, they realised that in order to exercise these rights, women needed special accommodations.

Chapter Practice

Objective Questions

• Multiple Choice Questions

1. The Concept of Liberty, Equality and Fraternity is borrowed from ....
(a) Russian Revolution   (b) Chinese Revolution
(c) French Revolution   (d) Japanese Revolution
Ans. (c) The Concept of Liberty, Equality and Fratenity is borrowed from French Revolution.

2. What is the powerful and political ideal that aims to ensure that everyone gets the same status?
(a) Faith   (b) Equality
(c) Liberty   (d) Justice
Ans. (b) Equality is a powerful moral and political ideal which aims to ensure that everyone gets the same status and rights in order to enjoy his life.

3. The concept of ...., as a political ideal, implies that all human beings are of equal value, regardless of their colour, gender, ethnicity or nationality.
(a) Liberty   (b) Freedom
(c) Equality   (d) Justice
Ans. (c)

4. From which of the following constitution we have borrowed the concept of 'Liberty, Equality and Fraternity'?
(a) USA Constitution   (b) South Africa Constitution
(c) Canada Constitution   (d) French Constitution
Ans. (d) The French revolutionaries used the slogan 'Liberty, Equality and Fraternity' to protest against the monarchy and the landed feudal aristocracy in the eighteenth century.

5. Which of the following inequalities cannot be altered?
(a) Social inequalities   (b) Natural inequalities
(c) Political inequalities   (d) Inherent inequalities
Ans. (b) It is assumed that natural inequalities cannot be altered.

6. Which of the following grounds creates discrimination among the society?
(i) Gender   (ii) Caste
(iii) Region   (iv) Religion
Select the correct options.
(a) (i), (ii) and (iii)   (b) (ii), (iii) and (iv)
(c) (i), (iii) and (iv)   (d) All of these
Ans. (d) Discrimination on the basis of gender, caste, region and religion, etc. are inequalities created by society.

7. Political equality, also known as equality before the law, is a vital first step toward equality, but it is also complemented by ....
(a) Social Inequalities
(b) Equality of opportunity
(c) Affirmative action
(d) Freedom of expression
Ans. (b) The concept of equality before law has been borrowed from the British Constitution and it is the first step towards equality and also complemented by equality of opportunity.

8. Select the wrong statement.
(a) Normal inequality and socially induced inequalities have been distinguished in political theory on occasion
(b) Natural inequalities are considered to be the result of the different characteristics and abilities with which people are born
(c) Social inequalities are those which are created by only an individual
(d) In democratic societies, political equality would normally include granting equal citizenship to all the members of the state
Ans. (c) Social inequalities are those which are created by only an individual.

9. When there are no significant differences in wealth, income and property between individuals or classes, then it leads to ....
(a) Political equality   (b) Economic equality
(c) Social equality   (d) All of these
Ans. (b) Economic equality

10. .... argued that the root cause of inequality in society was private ownership of economic resources.

(a) Stephen Hawking   (b) JS Mill
(c) Karl Marx   (d) John Locke

Ans. (c) It was Karl Marx who argued that the root cause of inequality in society was private ownership of economic resources.

11. Consider the following statements.

(i) A political doctrine which advocates unequal rights for women and men is called feminism.

(ii) According to Karl Marx inequality has come because of the private ownership and control of important economic resources like oil, land, forests and other forms of property.

Select the correct statements.

(a) Only (i)   (b) Only (ii)
(c) Both (i) and (ii)   (d) None of these

Ans. (b) A political doctrine which advocates equal rights for women and men is called feminism. Hence, statement (i) is incorrect.

Inequality has come because of the private ownership and control of important economic resources like oil, land, forests and other forms of property. Hence, statement (ii) is correct. Therefore, (b) is the correct option.

12. Which of the following statements is incorrect?

(a) Inequalities which are entrenched, that is, which remain relatively untouched over generations, are more dangerous for a society

(b) Feminism is a political philosophy that advocates for equal rights for men and women

(c) For liberals the principle of competition is the most just and efficient way of selecting candidates for jobs or admission to educational institutions

(d) None of the above

Ans. (d) All the statements give above are correct.

13. Consider the following statements regarding Socialism.

(i) Socialism aims to minimise existing inequalities and distribute resources justly.

(ii) Rammanohar Lohia was an eminent socialist.

(iii) Lohia gave the concept of Sapta Kranti.

Which of the following statement(s) is/are correct?

(a) Only (i)   (b) (i) and (ii)
(c) (ii) and (iii)   (d) All of these

Ans. (d) All the given statement are correct.

14. Which of the following inequalities have been protecting by customs and legal system?

(a) Economic   (b) Political
(c) Social   (d) All of these

Ans. (d) Social, economic and political inequalities all over the world have been protected by customs and legal system that prohibited some sections of society from enjoying certain kinds of opportunities and rewards.

15. On which among the following grounds, does Indian Constitution prohibits discrimination?

(a) Religion   (b) Caste
(c) Sex   (d) All of these

Ans. (d) There should not be any kind of discrimination on the ground of religion, caste, sex, place of birth or residence which is provided under Article 15 of the Constitution.

16. Which of the following is a form of reverse discrimination?

(a) Reservation   (b) Racial prejudices
(c) Patriarchy   (d) Both (a) and (b)

Ans. (d) Racial prejudices and reservation are the form of reverse discrimination and they continue to engage in activities that the equality principal challenges and opposes.

• Assertion-Reasoning MCQs

Directions (Q. Nos. 17-20) In the questions given below, there are two statements marked as Assertion (A) and Reason (R). Read the statements and choose the correct option.

Codes

(a) Both A and R are true and R is the correct explanation of A.

(b) Both A and R are true, but R is not the correct explanation of A.

(c) A is true, but R is false.

(d) A is false, but R is true.

17. **Assertion** (A) French revolutionaries used the slogan 'Liberty, Equality and Fraternity' to protest against the democracy.

Reason (R) During anti-colonial independence movements in Asia and Africa in the twentieth century, the demand for equality was also increased.

Ans. (d) Assertion is false, but Reason is true. French revolutionaries used the slogan 'Liberty, Equality and Fraternity' to protest against the monarchy. India has adopted liberty, equality and fraternity from the French Constitution.

18. **Assertion** (A) Natural inequalities are considered to be the result of the different characteristics and abilities with which people are born.

Reason (R) Social inequalities are created by society.

Ans. (b) Both A and R are correct, but R is not the correct explanation of A. There is no correlation between reason and assertion, they both belongs to different part.

19. Assertion (A) The provision of reservations or quotas for the poor in admissions to higher education or employment is unjust.

Reason (R) It denies other parts of society their right to equal care arbitrarily.

Ans. (a) Both A and R are correct and R is the correct explanation of A.

20. Assertion (A) The Constitutions of most of the democratic government around the world have incorporated to prohibit discrimination.

Reason (R) There should not be discrimination on the ground of religion, race, caste so that it can attain equality.

Ans. (a) Both the statements are correct and R is the correct explanation of A.

• Case Based MCQs

1. Read the passage and answer the questions that follow.

Critics of positive discrimination, particularly policies of reservations, thus invoke the principle of equality to argue against such policies. They contend that any provision of reservations or quotas for the deprived in admissions for higher education or jobs is unfair as it arbitrarily denies other sections of society their right to equal treatment. They maintain that reservations are a form of reverse discrimination and they continue with the practices that the principle of equality questions and rejects. Equality requires that all persons be treated alike and when we make distinctions between individuals on the basis of their caste or colour, we are likely to reinforce caste and racial prejudices. For these theorists, the important thing is to do away with social distinctions that divide our society.

(i) ………… is an act of giving advantage to those groups in society that are often treated unfairly because of their race, sex, caste, region or religion etc.

(a) Inequality
(b) Social discrimination
(c) Biased sociality
(d) None of the above

Ans. (b) Social discrimination

(ii) What is equality?

(a) Equality means that all persons be treated alike.
(b) Equality requires that distinctions between individuals on the basis of their caste or colour.
(c) Equality means dividing the society.
(d) All of the above

Ans. (a) Equality means that all persons be treated alike.

(iii) Why this passage suggests to do away with social distinction?

(a) Reinforcement of caste and racial prejudice
(b) Social distinction divides the society
(c) Both (a) and (b)
(d) Neither (a) nor (b)

Ans. (c) Both (a) and (b)

(iv) Positive discrimination questions the principle of …………… .

(a) Equality
(b) Inequality
(c) Criticism
(d) Sociality

Ans. (a) equality

(v) Consider the following statements.

1. There is no provisions of reservations or quotas for the deprived in admissions for higher education or jobs in our constitution.
2. Equality requires that all persons be treated alike.

Which of the statements given above is/are correct?

(a) Only 1
(b) Only 2
(c) Both 1 and 2
(d) None of these

Ans. (b) There is a provision for reservation in our constitution for deprived classes in admissions and jobs. Hence, statement 1 is incorrect.

Equality requires that all persons be treated alike. Hence, statement 2 is correct. Therefore, (b) is the correct option.

PART 2

Subjective Questions

• Short Answer Type Questions

1. What are the main features of equality?

Ans. Main features of equality are as follows

- Equality advocates an equitable and fair distribution of wealth and resources i.e. minimum possible gap between the rich and poor.
- Equality implies the system of equal and adequate opportunities for all the people in society.
- Equality affirms the grant and guarantee of equal rights and freedoms to all the people.
- Equality does not stand for absolute equality. It accepts the presence of some natural inequalities.

2. What do you understand by 'certain minimum conditions of life' in context of equality?

Ans. Equality means the state of being equal, especially in status, rights or opportunities. To achieve the objectives of equality certain minimum conditions are required to be provided to every member of the society.

Such minimum conditions refer to those conditions which are capable to live a dignified life. These conditions are adequate health facility, the opportunity for good education, adequate nutrition and a minimum wage, etc.

In the absence of such facilities it is exceedingly difficult for all the members of the society to compete on equal terms.

3. What are natural inequalities?

Ans. The most essential part of inequality is natural inequality. It is 'natural inequality,' such as disparities in colour, height and gender.

Natural inequalities are said to be the outcome of persons being born with different characteristics and skills. Natural differences must be acknowledged as equality because no man-made environment can be created and they cannot be altered or adjusted. Natural inequality exists when some people are black and others are white; similarly, natural inequality exists when one person is male and the other is female. These are passed down from generation to generation and are based on natural circumstances.

4. "Political equality or equality before the law is essential for us." Give your opinion on this statement.

Ans. Political equality or equality before the law is essential for us due to following reasons

- It grants equal citizenship to all members of the state.
- It ensures conditions which allow the citizens to participate in the affairs of the state.
- Political equality gives us certain rights such as Right to Vote, Right to Contest Elections, Right to Criticise the Government, etc.

These rights give opportunity to citizens to participate in the system of governance and decision-making.

5. How does the Indian Constitution ensure social equality?

Ans. Since ancient times, there have been stark socio-economic inequities in Indian society. Following independence, the Constitution authors safeguarded social equality by establishing the Fundamental Right to Equality, which forbids discrimination in public places on any social basis (Article 15).

The framers of the Constitution established equality before the law (Article 14) and discrimination on any social basis is illegal. Article 17 also abolishes the age-old practice of untouchability. Social equality is ensured in his path through this right.

6. "No society treats all its members in exactly the same way under all conditions." Explain this statement.

Ans. Equality is an ideal and practically, it is challenging to apply it. It means no society can treat all its members in

exactly the same way under all conditions. The smooth functioning of society requires division of work and functions and people often enjoy different status and rewards on account of it.

Many times, these differences of treatment may appear acceptable or even necessary. For example, we usually do not feel that giving Prime Ministers or army generals, a special official rank and status goes against the concept of equality, provided that their privileges are not misused.

7. "Patriarchy is based on the assumption that men and women are different by nature and this difference justifies their unequal positions in society." Comment on this statement based on your own experiences.

Ans. Patriarchy is the prime obstacle to women's advancement and development. Despite differences in levels of domination, the broad principles remain the same, i.e. men have the control. In the modern world where women go ahead by their merit, patriarchy creates these obstacles for women to go forward in society, because patriarchal institutions and social relations are responsible for the unequal positions of women in society.

Patriarchy refers to the male domination both in public and in private sphere. In this way, feminists use the term 'patriarchy' to describe the power relationship between men and women as well as to find out the root cause of women's subordination.

8. What are the seven kinds of inequalities identified by Rammanohar Lohia? **[NCERT]**

Ans. Eminent socialist thinker Rammanohar Lohia identified seven kinds of inequalities. These are
  (i) Inequality between man and woman,
  (ii) Inequality based on skin colour,
  (iii) Caste-based inequality,
  (iv) Colonial rule over some countries
  (v) Economic inequality
  (vi) Revolution for civil liberties against unjust encroachments on private life
  (vii) Revolution for Non-violence

These were the seven revolutions or Sapta Kranti which was the ideas of socialism for Lohia.

9. What steps can be taken to achieve formal equality?

Ans. Formal inequalities must be eliminated in order to attain formal equality in society. Formal inequality is analogous to an inflexible system founded on false assumptions that has gained credibility over time. As a result, in order to achieve legal equality, such misconceptions about some persons and privileged positions for others must be dispelled.

The law and government agencies should not support the powerful guy and vent purposes in which the old system is intentionally built-up in his favour. Discrimination on the basis of socioe-conomic status is forbidden in the Indian Constitution and untouchability is abolished.

10. Why do we need affirmative action?   **[NCERT]**

Ans. We need affirmative action because our society has entrenched (rooted) inequality. Customs in our society since ages has deprived lower castes to minimum standard of living. Due to their continuous deprivation, they have been made more backward. In India, there has been inadequate facilities to provide good schooling and health services to all sections of the society.

Government has taken affirmative action and provided them reservations and other privileges, so that they get a level playing field in competition and live a dignified life with other people.

11. How can affirmative action help in minimising social inequalities?

Ans. Indian society suffers from substantial inequalities in education, employment and income based on caste and ethnicity. Affirmative action help in minimising these sufferings or social inequalities in following ways

- It gives opportunities to socially and economically weaker sections of the society to enhance their talents and capabilities.
- It gives recognition to the needy people.
- It ensures minimum standard of living in society.
- It eliminates social prejudices from society.

12. Write the criticism of affirmative action.

Ans. By taking affirmative actions, Indian Government has given reservations to socially backward classes. Critics of affirmative action says that reservations go against the right to equal treatment. Those critics advocate that reservations are reverse discrimination.

Equality means that all persons should be treated equally and if we will make distinctions between castes to provide reservations in jobs, we will further reinforce the caste factor. So, they say that we need to do away with affirmative action.

13. Match the following concepts with appropriate instances.   **[NCERT]**

(i)	Affirmative action	(a)	Every adult citizen has a Right to Vote.
(ii)	Equality of Opportunity	(b)	Banks offer higher rate of interest to senior citizen.
(iii)	Equal Rights	(c)	Every child should get free education.

Ans. **Affirmative Action** Banks offer higher rate of interest to senior citizens. Appropriate instances after contributing for a long time in nation building process a person becomes senior citizen. It is generally considered that increasing age imposes several limitations on the elderly, biologically, socially and economically. To give them social security, banks offer higher rate of interest to senior citizen.

Equality of Opportunity Every child should get free education. Appropriate instances due to socio-economic backwardness, a number of children do not get opportunity of education. Thus, it should be ensured that every child should get free education.

Equal Rights Every adult citizen has a Right to Vote. Appropriate instances every citizen has right to enjoy political rights. Right to Vote is a good example of equal rights in our country.

• Long Answer Type Questions

1. How has the concept of equality influenced global political movements?

Ans. The concept of equality, as a political ideal, implies that all human beings are of equal value, regardless of their colour, gender ethnicity or nationality because of their shared nature.

There have been organised movements in various regions of the world whenever there has been a violation of equality and people have been exploited on the basis of uneven position and opportunities. The equality of human beings has been used as a rallying slogan in the campaigns against oppressive states and social, economic and religious organisations that promote and glorify inequalities of rank, status, sex and money since the inception of democratic governance systems. The French Revolution was a historic event in the eighteenth century and equality was the main gospel.

The movement's primary slogans were equality, fraternity and liberty. It was a reaction to the monarchy and the landed feudal elite. Anti-colonial movements in Asia, Africa and Latin America made equality a popular demand during the twentieth century. Untouchability with Indian Dalits was eradicated in the same spirit as abolition of racialism.

Inequality is most obvious around us around the world, notwithstanding these campaigns for equality. However, its popularity is growing.

2. Explain the three dimensions of equality.

Ans. Based on different kinds of inequalities which exist in society, there are three dimensions of equality i.e. Political, Social and Economic.

(i) **Political Equality** It includes granting equal citizenship to all the members of the state. The rights which are considered necessary to enable citizen to develop themselves and participate in the affairs of two state are right to vote freedom of expressions, movement and association and freedom of belief. These rights are also considered as legal rights, which are guaranteed by constitution and laws.

Even in countries where all people have equal rights, significant inequalities will occur. Inequalities in the social and economic worlds are often the product of disparities in the wealth and opportunities available to people. As a result, demands for fair rights or a 'level playing field' are often made.

(ii) **Social Equality** Making equal laws are not sufficient, as we require equality in the access of resources (social goods), the pursuit of equality requires that people belonging to different groups and communities also have a fair and equal chance to complete for those goods and opportunities.

So, there is a need for equal, social and economic conditions like adequate provision of health care, education, nutrition and minimum wages. Unequal opportunities do not arise only from lack of goods but also from customs.

(iii) **Economic Equality** When there is no significant differences in wealth, income and property between individuals or classes, then it leads to economic equality. Another method will be to measure the number of people living in poverty. Entrenched inequalities or those that have remained largely unchanged over centuries, are more detrimental to a community.

If certain groups of citizens in a society have accumulated significant wealth and the power that comes with it over centuries, the society will become divided between those classes and those who have remained poor.

3. What are the differences in the views of Karl Marx and liberals on equality?

Ans. **Views of Karl Marx on Equality**

Karl Marx, a 19th century thinker says that inequality has arisen because of the ownership of important economic resources like oil, land, forests and other forms of property by rich class. By owning such great economic power, they have also got hold of political power.

These rich classes make policies which are beneficial for rich class only and are disadvantageous to poor class. So, only providing opportunities will not help the poor class.

Karl Marx says that the need is to have state or public control over the resources and property of the society. He believes that social, economic and political inequalities are interlinked to each other because rich people having control over wealth leads to control over political system and this also makes them powerful in society.

Views of Liberals on Equality

Liberals believe that while state try to ensure a minimum standard of living and equal opportunities to all, this cannot by itself bring equality and notice to society. They opine that when people have attained minimum standard of living, they should be allowed to compete between them and then everybody will get

according to their hard work. As long as competition is there, inequalities will not be there in the system.

They believe that political, social and economic inequalities are not linked. They want each sphere to be dealt individually to tackle its problems. For political inequality we need democracy and for social and economic inequality, state can intervene to provide minimum standard of living. Liberals do not have problem, as such with inequality, but they want that inequality should not disturb us while achieving our capabilities.

4. What is Feminism? What are the views of feminism in the context of inequalities?

Ans. Feminism is a political doctrine of equal rights for women and men. Feminists are those men and women who believe that many of the inequalities we see in society between men and women are neither natural nor necessary and can be altered so that both women and men can lead free and equal lives.

Views of Feminism

- According to feminists, inequality between men and women in society is the result of patriarchy. This term refers to a social, economic and cultural system that values men more than women and gives men power over women.
- Patriarchy is based on the assumption that men and women are different by nature and that this difference justifies their unequal positions in society.

Feminists questions this way of thinking by making a distinction between 'sex' i.e., biological difference between men and women and 'gender' which determines the different roles that men and women play in society.

- Patriarchy produces a division of labour by which women are supposed to be responsible for 'private' and 'domestic' matters while men are responsible for work in the 'public' domain.
- Feminists question this distinction by pointing out that in fact most women are also active in the 'public' domain. That is, most women all over the world are employed in some form of work outside the home, but women continue to be solely responsible for housework as well.

5. What is socialism? Write about Rammanohar Lohia's view on equality.

Ans. Socialism refers to a set of political ideas that emerged as a response to the inequalities present in and reproduced by, the industrial capitalist economy.

The main concern of Socialism is how to minimise existing inequality and distribute resources justly. Although advocates of socialism are not entirely opposed to the market, they favour some kind of government regulation, planning and control over certain key areas such as education and health care.

In India the eminent socialist thinker Rammanohar Lohia, identified five kinds of inequalities that need to be fought against simultaneously.

Inequality between man and woman, inequality based on skin colour, caste-based inequality, colonial rule of some countries over others, and, of course, economic inequality.

This might appear a self-evident idea today. But during Lohia's time it was common for the socialists to argue that class inequality was the only form of inequality worth struggling against. Other inequalities did not matter or would end automatically if economic inequality could be ended.

Lohia argued that each of these inequalities had independent roots and had to be fought separately and simultaneously. He did not speak of revolution in the singular. For him struggle against these five inequalities constituted five revolutions.

He added two more revolutions to this list

- Revolution for civil liberties against unjust encroachments on private life.
- Revolution for non-violence, for renunciation of weapons in favour of Satyagraha.

These were the seven revolutions or Sapta Kranti which for Lohia was the ideal of socialism.

6. Some people argue that inequality is natural while others maintain that it is equality which is natural and the inequalities which we notice around us are created by society. Which view do you support? Give reasons. **[NCERT]**

Ans. To support or discard these arguments let us examine rationale behind it

Inequality is Natural People with this argument say that inequality is natural because people are not equal by birth because differ in traits, abilities and talents. Human beings differ in physical, mental and intellectual strength. There should be a division of work in society, as all people cannot do same work to be equal.

Inequality Created by Society People with this argument say that equality is natural but inequalities which we notice around us are created by society. Such as

- Unequal distribution of wealth and resources.
- Discrimination on the basis of gender, caste, region and religion, etc.
- Unequal opportunity of employment.

I support neither of the arguments because both arguments are valid in different circumstances. Inequalities which are natural can be bridged by giving special provisions to socially, economically as well as to physically challenged people.

• Case Based Questions

1. Read the passage and answer the questions that follow.

While reflecting on the issue of equality, a distinction must also be made between treating everyone in an identical manner and treating everyone as equals. The latter may on occasions need differential treatment but in all such cases the primary consideration is to promote equality. Differential or special treatment may be considered to realise the goal of equality but it requires justification and careful reflection. Since differential treatment for different communities was part and parcel of the caste system and practices like apartheid, liberals are usually very wary of deviations from the norm of identical treatment.

(i) What distinctions should be made while considering equality issues?

(ii) What would be the most important factor in treating everyone equally?

(iii) What conditions must be met in order for you to receive special treatment?

Ans. (i) While reflecting on the issue of equality, a distinction must also be made between treating everyone in an identical manner and treating everyone as equals.

(ii) Differential or special treatment may be considered to realise the goal of equality but it requires justification and careful reflection.

(iii) It requires justification and careful reflection.

2. Read the following source and answer the questions that follow.

The caste system in India prevented people from the 'lower' castes from doing anything except manual labour. The constitutions of most of the democratic government around the world have incorporated to prohibit discrimination on grounds of caste, race, sex, birth or religion…....many of these issues relating to the pursuit of equality have been raised by the women's movement. In the nineteenth century women struggled for equal rights. They demanded, for instance, the right to vote, the right to receive degrees in colleges and universities and the right to work....our constitution also abolishes the practice of untouchability. The idea of equality has been publicly adopted by most modern constitutions and democratic governments and it has been put into law as equal treatment for all citizens regardless of caste, race, religion or gender.

   (i) Which article talk about the abolition of untouchability?

   (ii) What were the most important demands made by the women's movement?

   (iii) What is equality?

Ans. (i) Our constitution also abolishes the practice of untouchability under Article 17.

   (ii) They demanded, for instance, the right to vote, the right to receive degrees in colleges and universities and the right to work.

   (iii) Equality means that all people are entitled to same rights and opportunities to develop their skills and to pursue their goals and ambitions.

3. Observe the cartoon given below and answer the questions that follow.

   (i) What does the above cartoon represent?

Ans. The above cartoon represents equality. For representing equality all the candidates are given same test.

   (ii) Do you think to ensure fair selection, same test should be conducted? Give arguments.

Ans. Fair selection depends on various factors. To conclude this question let us examine it from both point of view i.e., in favour and against it.

In Favour of View

• It gives equal opportunity to all competitors.

• It gives same playing field to all.

Against View

• It is not suitable for physically disadvantaged.

• It does not measure optimum capabilities of all competitors.

Thus, to ensure fair selection, it is better to bring everyone on equal level and then adopt the same process.

   (iii) Why is equality important for us?

Ans. Equality is important to get equal treatment and it cannot be discriminated on the basis of colour, race, gender, caste, religion and regions. This gives freedom to an individual to cherish dignity and respect in society.

Chapter Test

- **Objective Type Questions**

  1 What was the slogan of French Revolution?

     (a) Economic and Social Justice

     (c) Liberty, Equality and Fraternity

     (b) Political and Social Equality

     (d) Feminism, Socialism and Republicanism.

  2 Who among the following was an eminent socialist?

     (a) Rammanohar Lohia (b) John Locke,   (c) JS Mill   (d) Adam Smith

  3 .... refers to an ideology which values men more than women.

     (a) Socialism   (b) Feminism   (c) Patriarchy   (d) Matriarchy

  4 It includes granting equal citizenship to all the members of the state.
     Which of the following equality the given statements is talking about?

     (a) Political equality

     (c) Economic equality

     (b) Social equality

     (d) Both (a) and (c)

  5 What kind of rights is 'Right to vote'?

     (a) Constitutional Rights

     (c) Legal Rights

     (b) Fundamental Rights

     (d) Both (a) and (c)

- **Short Answer Type Questions**

  1 What are the three dimensions of equality?

  2 Write about paradox of equality.

  3 "Liberty and equality are complementary to each other." Explain.

  4 Who was Karl Marx? Write about his main thoughts on inequality.

  5 What are the positive and negative aspects of equality?

  6 Mention the difference between equality and uniformity.

  7 Define the concept of feminism.

- **Long Answer Type Questions**

  1 Describe in detail the economic equality.

  2 Distinguish between political and social equality.

  3 What is the relationship between liberty and equality?

  4 What is socialism? Write about Rammanohar Lohia's view on equality.

  5 "Political liberty is meaningless without economic equality." Elucidate.

CHAPTER 03

Justice

In this Chapter...

- Meaning of Justice
- Principles of Justice
- Different Dimensions of Justice
- Distributive Justice
- John Rawls' Theory of Justice
- Pursuing Social Justice

Meaning of Justice

Justice means fair treatment of people and the quality of being reasonable. Justice helps in the maintenance of a **just** and **rational** society. Justice is the proper administration of the law. It is the fair and equitable treatment of all individuals under the law. Justice was associated with Dharma in ancient Indian culture and upholding **Dharma** or just social order, was considered to be a primary duty of kings.

Chinese philosopher **Confucius** argued that king should maintain justice by "punishing wrong doers and rewarding the virtuous."

Plato in his book **The Republic** argued that "not to interfere in work area of others and to do our duties is justice". He examined why we should be concerned about justice.

According to **Socrates** "justice does not only mean doing good to our friends and harm to our enemies, or pursuing our own interests. Justice involves the well-being of all people."

According to the German philosopher **Immanuel Kant** "human beings possess dignity. If all persons are granted dignity then what is due to each of them is that they have the opportunity to develop their talents and pursure their chosen goals. Justice requires that we give due and equal consideration to all individuals."

Principles of Justice

To provide each person his/her equal importance, a number of different principles have been put forward which are as follows

Equal Treatment for Equals

One of the principles of justice is treating equals equally. All individuals have certain characteristics as human beings for which they deserve equal rights and treatment. For example, **right to life**, **liberty and property**, **right to vote**, which enable people to participate in political processes and certain social rights which would include the right to enjoy equal opportunities with other members of the society.

Apart from equal rights, the principle of treating equals equally also require that people should not be discriminated against on grounds of class, caste, race or gender. They should be judged on the basis of their work and actions and not on the basis of group to which they belong. As a result, if two people from different castes do the same job, they should be compensated equally.

Proportionate Justice

Justice is not solely based on the concept of fair treatment. There will be occasions where we believe that treating all fairly will be unfair. In such cases, fairness will mean rewarding individuals in proportion to the size and nature of their effort, assuming everyone begins from the same base line of equal rights.

Most people would agree that, while everyone should be paid the same for the same job, it would be reasonable and just to compensate different types of work differently based on factors like the amount of effort needed, the expertise required, the potential dangers involved in that job and so on.

If we use these parameters, we can find that some types of workers in our society are not paying a wage that adequately considers such factors. Miners, professional craftsmen and people in often risky yet socially useful occupations like police officers, for example, do not always receive a fair reward as compared to what others in society may be receiving. For justice in society, the principle of equal treatment needs to be balanced with the principle of proportionality.

Recognition of Special Needs

This principle recognise for a society to take into account special needs of people while distributing rewards or duties. This would be considered a way of promoting social justice. People with special needs or disabilities could be considered unequal in some particular respect and deserving of special help.

Physical disabilities, age or lack of access to good education or health care, are some of the factors which are considered grounds for special treatment in many countries. In our country, lack of access to good education or health care and other such facilities is often found combined with social discrimination on grounds of caste. Therefore, the Constitution allowed for reservations of government jobs and quotas for admissions to educational institutions for people belonging to the Scheduled Castes and Scheduled Tribes.

Our discussion of various principles of justice revealed that governments may find it difficult to reconcile the three principles of justice discussed: equal treatment for equals, consideration of different efforts and skills when assessing incentives and burdens, and provision of a minimum standard of living and equal opportunities to the needy. Pursuing equality of treatment by itself may sometimes work against giving due reward to merit.

Emphasising rewarding merit as the core principle of justice may result in marginalised groups being at a disadvantage in many places because they lack access to amenities such as good nutrition and education. Depending on which theory of justice they emphasise, different groups in the country can favour different policies. Governments must then harmonise the various values in order to promote a just society, otherwise they would be at a disadvantage in certain ways.

Different Dimensions of Justice

Different dimensions of Justice helps in creating a just society. **Legal, social, political and economic justice** are the key dimensions of justice. Here, we will try to understand these dimensions in some details.

Legal Justice

It is a narrow concept of justice which is associated with the legal system and legal procedure existing in a society. The court of law interprets the law and applies it after hearing the partners involved in a dispute. Here, justice is what administered by the **court of law** and the **interpretation of the judge** is considered to be an embodiment of justice.

Political Justice

In any democratic society political justice means providing **equal political rights**. Political justice stands for a free and fair participation of people in the political sphere. **Universal Adult Franchise**[1] is the expression of political justice. Equality of opportunity in getting elected and in holding public offices, freedom of expression and association are important pillars of political justice.

Social Justice

It means to end all types of social inequalities and to provide proper opportunity to every citizen in each sphere of life, to develop her/his personality to ensure equality of law, prohibition of discrimination, social security, provision of equal political rights, etc. The concept of social justice is based on the belief that all human beings are equal and no discrimination should be made on the ground of race, religion, caste gender and place of birth.

Economic Justice

It means to provide equal opportunities to everyone to earn her/his livelihood. It also means to help such people who are not able to work and earn their livelihood. The basic need of every person such as food, cloth, shelter and education should be fulfilled. It stands for by assuring adequate means of livelihood to all, by making provisions for fair distribution of resources, equal economic opportunity to all, etc.

While the concept of political justice is closely linked with the ideal of **liberty**, economic and legal justice with **equality** and social justice with **fraternity**, a just combination of all these four dimensions will help in achieving justice in life.

Just Distribution

To achieve social justice in society, governments might have to do more that just ensure that laws and polices treat individual in **fair manner**. A society requires just distribution of goods and services. If there are deep inequalities in society, then it requires redistribution of goods and resources.

As a result, social justice within a country would entail not just that people are treated equally in terms of the society's law and policies, but also that they have some basic equality in terms of life conditions and possibilities. This is seen to be vital for each individual to be able to follow his or her goals and express himself.

---

1. **Universal Adult Franchise** It refers that all citizens who are 18 years and above irrespective of their caste, religion, education, colour, race and economic conditions are free to vote".

For example, the Constitution abolished the **practice of untouchability** to promote social equality and ensure that people belonging to 'lower' castes have access to temples, jobs and basic necessities like water.

Different state governments have also taken some measures to redistribute important resources like, land in a more fair manner by instituting land reforms. Thus, distributive justice means that resources and goods should be distributed so that everybody can enjoy minimum quality of life. If everybody does not have **basic minimum resources**, then it should be redistributed from rich classes to poor classes.

John Rawls' Theory of Justice

There were some questions arising like type of society to choose, how people want to live in etc. John Rawls had tried to answer these questions.

John Rawl was an important **political thinker**, who has given a theory of justice to achieve a just state.

He claims that the only way to reach a fair and just law is to imagine ourselves in a situation where we must make decisions on how society should be organised while not knowing which role we will take in that society. We have no idea what kind of family we will be born into, whether we will be born into a 'upper' caste or 'lower' caste family, whether we will be born into a wealthy or poor family, privileged or deprived.

Rawls claims that if we don't know, who we'll be in the future and what choices we'll have, we'll be more likely to support a decision about the rules and organisation of that future community that is equal to all members.

He describes this as thinking under a **veil of Ignorance**. He expects that there could indeed be a rational justification for acknowledging the need to provide help to the least privileged members of a society.

Veil of Ignorance means that individuals are put in a position where they do not know their status, wealth, class, ability, talent, etc. So, these individuals will choose privileges which will affect them once they come out of veil of ignorance. The merit of the veil of ignorance position is that it expects people to just be their usual rational selves; they are expected to think for themselves and choose what they regard to be in their interest.

The pertinent thing however is that when they choose under the 'veil of ignorance' they will find that it is in their interest to think from the position of the worst-off.

It will be evident that rational persons will not only see things from the perspective of the worst-off, they will also try to ensure that the policies they frame benefit the society as a whole.

It would make sense if they also try to ensure that their chosen policy does not also make those who are better-off weaker because it is also possible that they could be born into a privileged position in the future society.

Therefore, it would be in the interests of all that society as a whole should benefit from the rules and policies that are decided and not just any particular section. Such fairness would be the outcome of rational action, not benevolence or generosity.

This is Rawls' theory of justice where rationality rather than moral thinking can lead us to have a fair and just society.

Pursuing Social Justice

Justice does not necessitate total equality and uniformity in how people live. However, a society is considered unequal if the disparities between rich and poor are so great that they seem to exist in parallel universes, and if the comparatively disadvantaged have no chance of improving their situation no matter how hard they work.

To put it another way, a just society should provide people with the **basic minimum conditions** to allow them to live safe, stable lives and grow their talents, as well as equal opportunities to achieve their desired goals in society.

Different governments and international organisations, such as the **World Health Organisation**, have developed various strategies for measuring people's basic needs.

However, it is generally understood that the basic amount of nutrition required to stay safe, shelter, access to clean drinking water, education, and a minimum wage are all essential components of these basic conditions. One of the duties of a **democratic government** is to meet the basic needs of its people.

In our country, different approaches are being supported by different political groups who debate the relative merits of different schemes for helping **marginalised sections** of the population, such as the rural or urban people.

Just Society

According to **BR Ambedkar**, a just society is that society in which ascending sense of respect and descending sense of disrespect is dissolved into the creation of a compassionate society.

Free Market vs State Intervention

Free market means that individuals should be free to own property and enter into contracts and agreements with each other regarding prices, wages and profits. They should be free to compete with each other to gain the greatest amount of benefit. This is a simple description of a free market.

Not all proponents of free markets today would support for completely unregulated markets. Many people are now willing to consider such restrictions; e.g. states could step into ensure that all people have a basic minimum standard of living so that they can compete on an equal terms.

But they might argue, that allowing markets to grow in health care, education, and other services is the most effective way of providing people with basic services.

One of the reasons for market distribution is that it provides us more options. Without a question, the business economy provides us with more options as customers. We have the freedom to choose what we eat and the school we attend, as long as we have the financial resources to do so.

Another common point in support of free markets and private enterprise is that the quality of services they provide is often superior to that of government institution. However, the expense of such facilities may be prohibitive for the vulnerable.

Private enterprise tends to go where it is most profitable, and therefore free markets tend to operate in the interests of the rich, affluent and powerful. Arguments may be made on both sides of the argument, but free markets often favour the already wealthy. This is why many argue that in order to ensure social justice, the government should intervene to ensure that basic services are provided to all members of society.

Disagreements about issues of distribution and justice are unavoidable and even healthy in a democratic society because they require us to consider other points of view and rationally defend our own views. Politics is all about resolving such differences through discussion.

Many types of **social** and **economic inequality** occur in our own country and much work remains to be done to reduce them. Studying the various concepts of justice should help us in debating the issues and reaching an agreement on the best course of action for seeking justice.

Chapter Practice

Objective Questions

• Multiple Choice Questions

1. ……… means fair treatment of people and the quality of being reasonable.
   (a) Equality   (b) Liberty
   (c) Fraternity   (d) Justice

Ans. (d) Justice means fair treatment of people and the quality of being reasonable.

2. Confucius was a philosopher who belonged to ……………… .
   (a) India   (b) China
   (c) Japan   (d) South Korea

Ans. (b) Confucius was a philosopher who belonged to China.

3. Which German philosopher argued that human beings possess dignity?
   (a) Socrates   (b) Plato
   (c) Immanuel Kant   (d) John Rawls

Ans. (c) According to the German philosopher Immanuel Kant "human beings possess dignity."

4. 'The Republic' argued that "to not interfere in work area of others and to do our duties is justice".

Whose word are given in the above statement?
   (a) Confucius   (b) Socrates
   (c) Plato   (d) Immanuel Kant

Ans. (c) Plato in his book 'The Republic' argued that "to not interfere in work area of others and to do our duties is justice".

5. Consider the following statements.
   (i) Immanuel Kant was an English Philosopher.
   (ii) According to Kant, justice requires that we give due and equal consideration to all individuals.

Which of the above statements is/are correct?
   (a) Only (i)   (b) Only (ii)
   (c) Both (i) and (ii)   (d) None of these

Ans. (b) According to German philosopher, Immanuel Kant, Justice requires that we give due and equal consideration to all individual.

6. Which of the following statements is incorrect?
   (a) Plato investigated why we should be concerned with justice.
   (b) Socrates tells young people that if everyone is unfair, no one will profit from injustice.
   (c) According to the German philosopher Immanuel Kant, human beings possess dignity.
   (d) Justice requires that we should not give due and equal consideration to all individuals.

Ans. (d) Justice requires that we should not give due and equal consideration to all individuals.

7. Which one of the following is not the principles of justice?
   (a) Treating equals equally
   (b) Treating unequal equally
   (c) Recognition of special needs
   (d) Proportionate justice

Ans. (b) One of the principles of justice is 'treating equals equally.' All individuals have certain characteristics as human beings for which they deserve equal rights and treatment.

8. They should be judged on the basis of their ……… .
   (a) group to which they belong
   (b) work and actions
   (c) region
   (d) Both (a) and (c)

Ans. (b) They should be judged on the basis of their work and actions and not on the basis of group to which they belong or not.

9. Consider the following statements.
   (i) Justice is solely based on the concept of fair treatment.
   (ii) The principle of fair treatment must be matched with the principle of proportionality in order for society.

Which of the following statement is/are correct?
   (a) Only (i)
   (b) Only (ii)
   (c) Both (i) and (ii)
   (d) None of the above

Ans. (b) Justice is not solely based on the concept of fair treatment. The principle of fair treatment must be matched with the principle of proportionality in order for society.

10. The principle of fair treatment must be matched with the .... in order for society to be justly.
(a) recognition of special needs (b) justful distribution
(c) principle of proportionality (d) free market intervention

Ans. (c) The principle of fair treatment must be matched with the principle of proportionality in order for society to be just.

11. Apart from equal rights, the principle of treating equals fairly requires that individuals not be discriminated against on the basis of class, caste, race or gender. They should be evaluated based on their ....
(a) wages (b) job and behaviour
(c) work experience (d) qualifications and skills

Ans. (b) Apart from equal rights, the principle of treating equals fairly requires that individuals not be discriminated against on the basis of class, caste, race or gender. They should be evaluated based on their job and behaviour.

12. Which of the following are key dimensions of justice?
(i) Legal Justice (ii) Emotional Justice
(iii) Political Justice (iv) Economic Justice

Select the correct options.
(a) (i) and (ii) (b) (ii), (iii) and (iv)
(c) (i), (iii) and (iv) (d) All of these

Ans. (c) Legal, social, political and economic justice are the key dimensions of justice.

13. Which of the following is not an expression of political justice?
(a) Universal adult franchise (b) Social inequalities
(c) Upholding dharma (d) Both (b) and (c)

Ans. (a) Universal adult franchise is the expression of political justice.

14. Which type of society is mentioned by B.R. Ambedkar?
(a) Distributive Society (b) Just Society
(c) Horticultural society (d) Industrial Society

Ans. (b) B.R. Ambedkar mentioned about the Just Society. According to him a Just society is that society in which ascending sense of reverence and descending sense of contempt is dissolved into the creation of a compassionate society.

15. The term 'Veil of Ignorance' is attributed to ....
(a) Socrates (b) BR Ambedkar
(c) John Rawls (d) Immanuel Kant

Ans. (c) The term 'Veil of Ignorance' is attributed to John Rawls

16. Consider the following statements.
(i) Free markets are required to ensure fair distribution of goods.
(ii) State intervention in markets is required so that quality goods and services can be provided.

Which of the above statements is/are correct?
(a) Only (i) (b) Only (ii)
(c) Both (i) and (ii) (d) None of the above

Ans. (d) Free markets are required so that quality goods and services can be provided. Hence, statement 1 is incorrect.
State intervention in markets is required to ensure fair distribution of goods. Hence, statement 2 is incorrect.
Therefore, options (d) is correct answer.

• Assertion-Reasoning MCQs

Directions (Q. Nos. 17-20) In the questions given below, there are two statements marked as Assertion (A) and Reason (R). Read the statements and choose the correct option.

Codes
(a) Both A and R are true and R is the correct explanation of A.
(b) Both A and R are true, but R is not the correct explanation of A.
(c) A is true, but R is false.
(d) A is false, but R is true.

17. Assertion (A) According to Chinese philosopher Confucius "justice does not only mean doing good to our friends and harm to our enemies or pursuing our own interests. Justice involves the well-being of all people".

Reason (R) Justice was associated with Dharma in ancient Indian culture and upholding Dharma was considered a primary duty of kings.

Ans. (d) A is false, but R is true. According to Socrates "justice does not only mean doing good to our friends and harm to our enemies or pursuing our own interests. Justice involves the well-being of all people".

18. Assertion (A) The Constitution allowed for reservations of government jobs and quotas for admissions to educational institutions for people belonging to the Scheduled Castes and Scheduled Tribes.

Reason (R) In our country, lack of access to good education or health care and other such facilities is often found combined with social discrimination on grounds of caste.

Ans. (a) Both A and R are correct and R is the correct explanation of A.

19. Assertion (A) The concept of legal justice is based on the belief that all human beings are equal and no discrimination should be made on the ground of race, religion, caste gender and place of birth.

Reason (R) Political justice stands for a free and fair participation of people in the political sphere.

Ans. (d) A is false, but R is true. The concept of social justice is based on the belief that all human beings are equal and no discrimination should be made on the ground of race, religion, caste gender and place of birth.

20. Assertion (A) In spite of the fact that Rawls theory has strong procedural features it can also be seen as a major contribution to social justice.

Reason (R) He is categorical that there is a need for rational justification of all departures from equality.

Ans. (a) Both A and R are true and R is the correct explanation of A.

• Case Based MCQs

1. Read the passage and answer the questions that follow.

Differences of opinion on matters such whether and how, to distribute resources and ensure equal access to education and jobs arouse fierce passions in society and even sometimes provoke violence. People believe the future of themselves and their families may be at stake. We have only to remind ourselves about the anger and even violence which has sometimes been roused by proposals to reserve seats in educational institutions or in government employment in our country. As students of political theory however we should be able to calmly examine the issues involved in terms of our understanding of the principles of justice.

(i) What is the ultimate result of differences of opinion on matters of distribution of resources?

(a) Fierce passion in society

(b) It can provoke violence

(c) Both (a) and (b)

(d) Neither (a) nor (b)

Ans. (c) Differences of opinion on matters such whether and how, to distribute resources and ensure equal access to education and jobs arouse fierce passions in society and even sometimes provoke violence.

(ii) ………… wanted to reveal in this passage that there should be a rational justification for acknowledging the need to provide help to the least privileged members of a society.

(a) Immanuel Kant   (b) John Rawls

(c) Plato   (d) Socrates

Ans. (b) John Rawls

(iii) What is a narrow concept of justice which is associated with the legal system and legal procedure existing in a society?

(a) Political justice   (b) Social justice

(c) Legal justice   (d) Economic justice

Ans. (c) Legal justice

(iv) Which of the following is required to balance a equal treatment?

(a) State intervention   (b) Political justice

(c) Proportionality   (d) None of these

Ans. (c) The equal treatment should be balanced by proportionality.

(v) Consider the following statements.

1. Justice ensures equal access to education and jobs arouse fierce passions in society.

2. It can also provoke violence.

Which of the statements given above is / are correct?

(a) Only 1   (b) Only 2

(c) Both 1 and 2   (d) None of these

Ans. (c) Both the statements are correct.

PART 2
Subjective Questions

• Short Answer Type Questions

1. What is justice? What is the view of Socrates on Justice?

Ans. Justice means fair treatment of people and the quality of being reasonable is the proper administration of the law and the fair and equitable treatment of all individuals under the law. Justice helps in the maintenance of a just and rational society.

According to Socrates, "justice does not only mean doing good to our friends and harm to our enemies or pursuing our own interests. Justice involves the well-being of all people. "

2. Does the principle of considering the special needs of people conflict with the principle of equal treatment for all?   **[NCERT]**

Ans. The principle of considering the special needs of people does not raise a conflict with the principle of equal treatment for all because

• People with special needs are given special treatment to facilitate their participation in the running of the society.

• People with special needs also require special treatment for integration with society and for securing opportunities and basic needs that would be otherwise denied to them.

• The senior citizens, women and socially backward people are given special treatment due to their special needs.

3. What do you mean by 'just distribution of resources'?

Ans. A society requires just distribution of goods and services for maintaining law and order. If there are deep inequalities in society, then it requires redistribution of goods and resources. For example, when India was under

British rule, then zamindars had acquired vast areas of land. But after independence, land reforms were introduced and land was redistributed among poor peasants.

If everybody does not have education, then open Civil Services Examination does not have any value because only highly educated people can take examinations then.

Thus, just distribution means that resources and goods should be so distributed that everybody can enjoy minimum quality of life. If everybody does not have basic minimum resources, then it should be redistributed from rich classes to poor classes.

4. Explain the concept of protective discrimination.

Ans. Protective discrimination is the policy of granting special privileges to the downtrodden and the underprivileged sections of society, most commonly women and socially weaker classes. Some of the citizens are depressed due to discriminatory social practices prevalent in the past and such a depression has hampered their right to basic dignified life.

They are considered to be a case fit for being treated preferentially. For example, the constitution allowed for reservations of government jobs and quotas for admissions to educational institutions for people belonging to the Scheduled Castes and Scheduled Tribes.

5. What are three different dimensions of Justice? Explain Legal Justice.

Ans. Different dimensions of Justice helps in creating a just society. Legal, social, political and economic justice are the key dimensions of justice.

Legal Justice It is a narrow concept of justice which is associated with the legal system and legal procedure existing in a society. The court of law interprets the law and applies it after hearing the partners involved in a dispute. Here, justice is what administered by the court of law and the interpretation of the judge is considered to be an embodiment of justice.

6. 'Social justice is lacking in society'. Justify this statement with your real-life experiences.

Ans. Social justice is based on the value of fairness, equality, respect for diversity, access to social protection and the application of human rights in all spheres of life, including in the work place. In society, lack of social justice is noticeable in every sphere of life such as distribution of resources, disrespect towards weaker and tribal people and women. On one hand, some people enjoy too much power, while on the other hand rights of deprived people are suppressed.

7. What do you mean by distributive justice?

Ans. Distributive justice is concerned with the fair distribution of the burdens and benefits of social cooperation among diverse persons with competing needs and chaims. The modern framework of socio-economic ties among society's members is the foundation for distributive

justice. It is based on the assumption that the system contains a variety of rewards and advantages for various opportunities.

They should be divided in accordance with the people's merit and abilities. Positions in society are dispersed and should be distributed according to their value. The concept of justice is based on this. It also implies that social goods and responsibilities are shared among society's many members.

8. Which conditions in India have affected the minimum standard of life needed by people?

Ans. Continuous increase in India's population and the growth of the population residing in slums and small towns, has resulted in over-straining of infrastructure and a deterioration in public health. Inadequate civic amenities, lack of purchasing power and lack of knowledge and awareness among the poor have resulted in grave poverty.

A few government policies have specifically targeted the poor, but they have proved neither sufficient nor effective. The deteriorating health status of people in many parts of country needs urgent attention because many of recent health problems have potential to take an epidemic form if neglected. A resurgence of malaria, dengue and tuberculosis indicates that much of the poor health emanates (arise) from a lack of basic amenities such as sanitation, clean water and housing, coupled with a precautionary measure against preventable and infectious diseases.

9. Explain the concept of free market.

Ans. Free market means that individuals should be free to own property and enter into contracts and agreements with each other regarding prices, wages and profits. They should be free to compete with each other to gain greatest amount of profit. It is argued, if free markets are left free of state interference, then the sum of market transactions would ensure overall a just distribution of benefits and duties in society.

Now a days, free markets are demanding state to step in to regulate markets like provision of healthcare and education. Free market also allows us to have more choices and moreover, they provide good quality services in comparison to poor quality of services provided by government institutions. But free markets favor the privileged because they have money and resources to buy goods and services they want.

10. What are the advantages and disadvantages of free markets?

Ans. Advantages of free market are
- In free markets, there is less interference by state which ensures equal distribution of benefits and duties in society.
- Free markets allow us to have more choices. They also provide us good quality of goods and services.

Disadvantage of free market are

- Free markets favour the privileged because they have money and resources to buy goods and services they want
- Profit maximisation is the biggest motivation for firm. In a free market, firms may try to reduce their costs unethically by polluting the environment or by exploiting workers.

11. 'Justice delayed is justice denied'. Justify the statement and give suggestions for fast redressal of justice.

Ans. 'Justice delayed is justice denied' is an old saying, which means that if timely justice is not provided to the sufferer, it loses its importance and violates human rights. The Indian judicial system still lives in old age. It has been observed that a number of cases are pending in courts for a very long time.

Following are the suggestions for fast redressal of justice

- Number of judges should be increased.
- All existing vacancies should be filled immediately.
- Artificial intelligence system should be introduced in court of law which would accelerate the process of administration of justice and also aid in giving flawless justice, thereby reducing the need of appeal.

12. "Justice implies something which is not only right to do and wrong to do; but which some individual person can claim from us as his moral right." Comment on this statement given by JS Mill.

Ans. This statement of Mill is based on Utilitarian theory of justice

- Utilitarian see justice as part of morality and don't see justice to have a higher priority than any other moral concern.
- Utilitarian ideas of justice connect morality to the law, economic distribution and politics.
- For justice, Mill argued that we should reduce the division between workers and owners.
- Workers and owners often engage in class warfare or other hostile relations.

This might be a way for workers and owners to be blend together rather than be sharply divided groups which could reduce class warfare and hostile relations. For example, profits could be shared with the workers.

• Long Answer Type Questions

1. Briefly discuss the three principles of justice outlined in this chapter. Explain each with examples.

Ans. The three principles of Justice are

(i) **Equal Treatment for Equals**

- This indicates the principle of treating people equally.

- All individuals share certain characteristics as human beings. Therefore, they deserve to be treated equally and equal rights should be provided.
- It includes civil rights like right to life, liberty and property, political rights like right to vote and social rights related to equal social opportunities.
- It also prohibits discrimination on the grounds of class, caste, gender and race. For example, two individuals from different backgrounds should be paid same reward for the same kind of job.

(ii) **Proportionate Justice**

- This principle indicates rewarding people in proportion to the scale and quality of their effort.
- It is just to reward different jobs differently on the basis of efforts, skills required and the danger involved.
- Proportionality provides balance to the principle of equal treatment. For example, the reward and compensation for a surgeon and an architect varies according to their skills which are required in their job.

(iii) **Recognition of Special Needs**

- This principle is based on distributing rewards and duties on the basis of special needs of people. On the basis of factors such as age, physical disabilities, and lack of access to good education or health care, special treatment is given in many countries.
- People with special needs or disabilities are treated unequal in some particular respect and therefore, are provided with some deserving and special help. A physically challenged person getting a reserved seat is an example of principle of recognition of special needs.

2. How does the Constitution of India promote the concept of social justice?

Ans. The Constitution of India has solemnly promised to all its citizens justices. Social, economic and political. The notion of justice is most commonly associated with an underlying assumption that justice equates to equal rights, access and fair treatment in the legal system. The concept of social justice is the necessary implication of welfare state. The scheme of social justice is very well incorporated in the various provisions of the Indian Constitution.

The Preamble of the Constitution includes the term like 'Socialist', 'Social and Economic Justices', 'Equality', etc, which specify that the state would extensively involve in social welfare of people and would try to establish a democratic society. Moreover, a distinct chapter of Directive Principles of State Policy has been dedicated towards the welfare responsibilities of the government, which lays down the norms of ideal governance of people's welfare.

Article 39 of the Constitution says that the state shall secure that the operation of the legal system promotes justice, on the basis of equal opportunity and shall, in particular provide free legal aid, by suitable legislation or schemes or in any other way, to ensure that opportunities for securing justice are not denied to any citizen by reason of economic or other disabilities.

Various Fundamental Rights and its subsequent amendments also intended to ensure social justice to the disadvantaged citizens.

3. What measures would you suggest to ensure social justice in India?

Ans. Social Justice in India can be ensured in the following ways

By Promotion of Equality Social Justice and human rights have some shared goal-human dignity and equality for all. The issues that make social justice difficult to achieve are-poverty, exclusion and discrimination. Thus, social justice can be ensured by promoting equality.

By Promotion of Welfare Systems In society many people are socially and economically deprived. They can be ensured justice by promoting welfare systems-such as housing support, food security, free health services, free education, etc.

By Giving Employment Rights Equal distribution of wealth is a cornerstone of social justice.
Equal sharing of wealth can be enhanced through equal opportunity of employment.

By Government Accountability Human rights provide a legal framework that allows individuals to hold government accountable and requires the state to create conditions necessary for the achievement of social justice.

By Implementation of Constitutional Provisions The Constitution of India provides many provisions to ensure social justice. But, due to lack of political will these Provisions are not implemented in its spirit. Thus, these provisions should be implemented to ensure social justice.

4. What are generally considered to be the basic minimum requirements of people for living a healthy and productive life? What is the responsibility of governments in trying to ensure this minimum to all?

Ans. Housing, supply of clean water, basic amount of nourishment, education and minimum wage are the basic minimum requirements of people for living a healthy and productive life. Government is responsible for providing these services to all sections of the society irrespective of their class, caste, race and gender at a cost they can afford. The responsibility of government in trying to ensure this minimum to all are

- Government should encourage private agencies to provide services such as health care, education, etc. and make policies that should try to empower people to buy those services.
- It might also be necessary for the government to give special help to the old and the sick who cannot compete.
- It should make availability of good quality goods and services at a cost people can afford.
- It should maintain a framework of law and regulations to ensure that competition between individuals remains free of coercion and other obstacles in market.

- In India, different approaches are being suggested by different political groups who debate the relative merits to help marginalised sections of people.

5. How does Rawls use the idea of veil of ignorance to argue that fair and just distribution can be defended on rational grounds?   **[NCERT]**

Ans. Rawls uses the ideal of a Veil of Ignorance to argue that fair and just distribution can be defended on rational grounds in following manners

- He says that if a person keeps himself/herself under the Veil of Ignorance then he/she would come up with the just distribution, fair laws and policies that would affect the whole society.
- A person under the Veil of Ignorance is unaware of his/her possible position and status in the society, therefore, he/she would rationally decide from the point of view of the worst-off.
- It would be sensible is this situation for everyone to ensure that all resources are available equally to all persons.
- It will be clear to a person who can reason and think for himself, that those who are born privileged will enjoy certain special opportunities.
- It would make sense for each person, acting in his or her own interest, to try to think of rules of organisation that will ensure reasonable opportunities to the weaker sections.
- In this way, Rawls with his idea of 'Veil of Ignorance' is able to prove that fair and just distribution can be defended on rational grounds with the help of this idea.

• Case Based Questions

1. Read the passage and answer the questions that follow.

Justice means fair treatment of people and the quality of being reasonable…. "Human beings possess dignity. If all persons are granted dignity, then what is due to each of them is that they have the opportunity to develop their talents and pursue their chosen goals. Justice requires that we give due and equal consideration to all individuals"…. One of the principles of justice is 'treating equals equally.' All individuals have certain characteristics as human beings for which they deserve equal rights and treatment.

(i) Whose words are there in above passage?

(ii) What do you mean by justice?

(iii) What does equal treatments for equal means?

Ans. (i) These are German philosopher Immanuel Kant's words.

(ii) Justice means fair treatment of people and the quality of being reasonable.

(iii) One of the principles of justice is 'treating equals equally.' All individuals have certain characteristics as human beings for which they deserve equal rights and treatment.

2. Read the following source and answer the questions that follow.

Differences of opinion on matters such whether and how, to distribute resources and ensure equal access to education and jobs arouse fierce passions in society and even sometimes provoke violence. People believe the future of themselves and their families may be at stake. We have only to remind ourselves about the anger and even violence which has sometimes been roused by proposals to reserve seats in educational institutions or in government employment in our country. We will discuss the theory of just distribution put forward by the well-known political philosopher, John Rawls. Rawls has argued that there could indeed be a rational justification for acknowledging the need to provide help to the least privileged members of a society.

(i) What was the issue on which violence will be evoked?

(ii) What does John Rawls have to say about it?

(iii) Who is well-known political philosopher?

Ans. (i) On the issue of distribution of resources and to ensure equal access to education and jobs.

(ii) Rawls has argued that there could indeed be a rational justification for acknowledging the need to provide help to the least privileged members of a society.

(iii) John Rawls.

3. Observe the cartoon given below and answer the questions that follow.

(i) What do you mean by Rule of law?

(ii) Do you think that the statue of justice blind folded symbolise impartial judgement? Give your view.

(iii) What are the three principles of Justice?

Ans. (i) Rule of law means that people are ruled by impersonal law and not by the personal rule of a man.

(ii) Blind justice is the theory that law should be viewed objectively with the determination of innocence or guilt made without bias or prejudice. The statue of justice holds balance scales, which represent the weighing of evidence; weighs the factors of a case to render a verdict. The scales imply a mechanistic, rational process; too much weight (evidence) on one side will cause the scales to tilt in favour of innocence or guilt. The origin of the blindfold is unclear, but there is some evidence that early artists added the blindfold to indicate the tolerance.

But today, the blindfold represents objectivity that justice is or should be delivered objectively without fear, passion or prejudice regardless of money, wealth, power or identity; blind justice and impartiality.

(iii) Three principles of Justice are as follows

* Equal treatment for equals.
* Proportionate Justice.
* Recognition of special needs.

4. Observe the cartoon given below and answer the questions that follow.

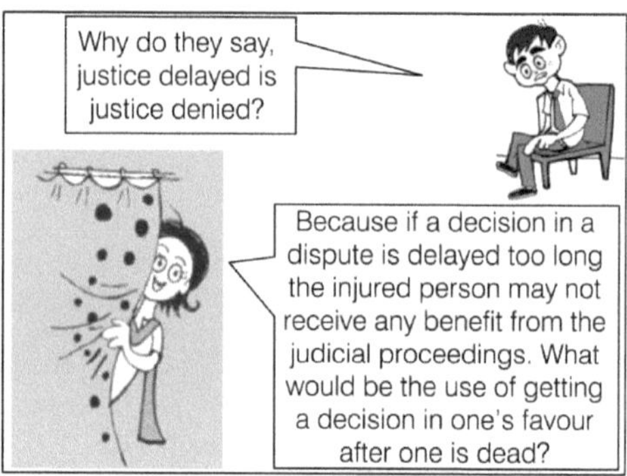

(i) How is Justice delayed is Justice denied?

(ii) What do you mean by a just society?

(iii) What is protective discrimination?

Ans. (i) 'Justice delayed is justice denied' is an old saying. It means that if timely justice is not provided to the sufferer, it loses its importance and violates human rights. The Indian Judicial System still lives in old age. It has been observed that a number of cases are pending in courts for a very long time. Following are the suggestions for fast redressal of justice

* Number of judges should be increased.
* All existing vacancies should be filled immediately.

(ii) A just society is that society in which ascending sense of respect and descending sense of disrespect is dissolved into the creation of a compassionate society.

(iii) Protective discrimination is a policy of granting special privileges to the downtrodden and the underprivileged sections of society.

Chapter Test

- ## Objective Type Questions

    1. Who said that justice involves non-interfearence in work areas of otehrs?
        - (a) Plato
        - (b) Ambedkar
        - (c) Kant
        - (d) Aristotle
    2. Which of the following shuld be included in the list of Equal rights for all?
        - (a) Right to life
        - (b) Right to property
        - (c) Right to vote
        - (d) All of these
    3. In Ancient Indian society, justice was associated with ....
        - (a) Moksha
        - (b) Dharma
        - (c) Astha
        - (d) None of these
    4. It means to provide equal opportunities to everyone to earn her/his livelihood.

       What does 'it' refer to in the above statement?
        - (a) Social justice
        - (b) Legal justice
        - (c) Economic justice
        - (d) Political justice
    5. Arrange the following in chronological order.

       The concept of political justice, economic and legal justice and social justice are linked with the ideals of
        - (a) fraternity, liberty, equality
        - (b) equality, fraternity, liberty
        - (c) liberty, equality, fraternity
        - (d) liberty, fraternity, equality

- ## Short Answer Type Questions

    1. What are BR Ambedkar's views on just society?
    2. What are contribution of reservation in promoting social justice?
    3. Write the essence of state intervention in market.
    4. Is justice all about fairness? Explain your views with examples.
    5. What do you mean by social justice? To what extent India has implemented it? Explain with examples.
    6. Which institution in our country has abolished untouchability?
    7. Give two examples of treating equals equally.

- ## Long Answer Type Questions

    1. Do you think that state intervention is good option for newly independent countries? Give reasons in support of your answer.
    2. Explain the significance of the statue of justice depicted as blindfolded figure.
    3. Write a note on Marxist's view of justice.

Practice Paper 1*
(Solved)

General Instructions

■ Time : 2 Hours
■ Max. Marks : 40

1. There are 10 questions in the question paper. All questions are compulsory.
2. Question no. 1 is a Case Based Question, which has five MCQs. Each question carries 1 mark.
3. Question no. 2-6 are Short Type Questions. Each question carries 3 marks.
4. Question no. 7-10 are Long Answer Type Questions. Each question carries 5 marks.
5. There is no overall choice. However, internal choice have been provided in some questions.
   Students have to attempt only on of the alternatives in such questions

** As exact Blue-print and Pattern for CBSE Term II exams is not released yet. So the pattern of this paper is designed by the author on the basis of trend of past CBSE Papers. Students are advised not to consider the pattern of this paper as official. It is just for practice purpose.*

Case Based MCQs

1. Read the given passage and answer the questions that follow.

The Supreme Court of India possesses advisory jurisdiction, which means that the President of India has the authority to refer any matter of public interest or involving constitutional interpretation to the Supreme Court for advice. Decisions made by Supreme Court are binding on other courts within the territory of India and are also enforceable throughout the length and breadth of the country. It allows the government to seek Legal opinion on a matter of importance before taking action on it. This may prevent unneccessary litigations later. Secondly, the government can make suitable changes in its actions of legislation in the light of the advice of Supreme Court. The Supreme Court itself is not bound by its decision and can review it anytime as prescribed by the provisions of the Constitution. The Supreme Court shall have power to review any judgement pronounced or order made by it.   (5×1 = 5)

(i) What are the different types of jurisdiction the supreme could have?
   (a) Advisory   (b) Appleate   (c) Original   (d) All of these

(ii) Which of the following body has the authority to refer any matter of public interest to the Supreme Court?
   (a) Parliament   (b) President   (c) Prime Minister   (d) High Court

(iii) Which Article of the Indian Constitutions deals with the power to review judgement made by the apex court?
   (a) Article 137   (b) Article 131   (c) Article 147   (d) Article 138

(iv) The Supreme Court's decisions are ………… by all Indian courts.
   (a) Enforceable   (b) Not enforceble   (c) Separate   (d) Both (a) and (c)

(v) Consider the following statements:

1. The Supreme Court, is bound to provide advice on such matter as reffered by the President.
2. The President is not obligated to take such advice as reffered by the Supreme Court.

Select the correct statement(s).

(a) Only 1   (b) Only 2   (c) Both (1) and (2)   (d) None of these

Short Answer Type Questions

2. Should Rajya Sabha be scrapped?   3 Marks

Or Why can the Lok Sabha control the executive more effectively than the Rajya Sabha?

3. What are the executive functions of the Indian President?   3 Marks

Or The Parliamentary system of executive vests many powers in the legislature for controlling the executive. Why do you think is it necessary to control the executive?

4. What do you mean by 'social constraints'? Is it necessary to have any form of restrictions in order to enjoy freedom?   3 Marks

5. What does Immanuel Kant say about justice? Mention any two postulates of Justice.   3 Marks

6. What are three different dimensions of Justice? Explain Legal and Economic Justice.   3 Marks

Or Distinguish between the 'Liberalists' and 'Marxists' views of justice.

Long Answer Type Questions

7. Discuss the Indian Parliament's powers and reason for decline.   5 Marks

Or What are the different functions of the Parliament?

8. What is Parliamentary Form of Government and Semi-Presidential form of Government? Why India adopted a Parliamentary system?   5 Marks

9. "No idea is completely false. What appears to us as false has an element of truth." Justify this statement in context of freedom.   5 Marks

Or What is liberalism? How is liberalism associated with freedom? What are Subhash Chandra Bose's thoughts on freedom?

10. Discuss what is Feminism and why it is important?   5 Marks

Or Define Socialism? Describe the socialist perspective on equality.

Answers

Case Based MCQs

1. (i) (d),   (ii) (b), (iii) (a),   (iv) (a),   (v) (b)

Short Answer Type Questions

2. The Rajya Sabha is Parliament's upper house. It is regarded as the permanent house since it does not dissolve. It is referred to as the State Council since it represents the interests of the States.

The Rajya Sabha is considered a useless and superfluous chamber because of its weaknesses in a number of areas such as legislative, financial and executive power. As a result, it should be abolished. However, this demand or idea is without merit for the following reasons

- India is governed by a federal structure, which necessitates the presence of an upper chamber in Parliament (Legislature).
- In a variety of ways, the Rajya Sabha and the Lok Sabha are equal.

- In various areas, the Rajya Sabha has extraordinary authority.
- It is the home of the wise and experienced.

Or Lok Sabha exercises control over the executive more effectively than Rajya Sabha because

- It is a directly elected body.
- The Council of Ministers is responsible to Lok Sabha and not the Rajya Sabha.
- The Lok Sabha has the power to make laws, ask question and amend the Constitution.
- The Lok Sabha can remove the government by expressing no-confidence motion but Rajya Sabha cannot remove any government.
- The Lok Sabha has crucial power in controlling the finances, as it can reject money bill but Rajya Sabha cannot.

3. The executives functions of the President are as follows

- The President can make rules specifying the manner in which the orders and the other instruments which are made and executed in his name shall be authenticated.
- The President appoints the Prime Minister and other Ministers, the Attorney General of India and determines his remuneration, the Governors of the States, Comptroller and Auditor General of India, Chief Election Commissioner and other Election Commissioners, Chairman and Members of the Union Public Service Commission, and Finance Commission of India Chairman and Members Judges of High Court and Supreme Court.
- The President shall also have the power to remove his Ministers, individually; Attorney-General of India; the Governors of the States.
- The Chairman or a Member of the Public Service Commission of the Union or of a State, on the report of the Supreme Court.

Or It is necessary for the legislature to control the executive because

- To ensure its accountability to the legislature.
- The various mechanisms ensures that the executive is answerable and controlled by the people's representatives so that there is transparency and accountability.
- The control on the executive is must so that it work according to the laws and checks deviation of any kind.
- It also prevents the domination of personality cult and provides a check on arbitrary functioning and concentration of power into a single source.

4. The domination and external controls on freedom of individual imposed by the society is known as social constraints. These controls may be imposed by the government through laws or constitution which embody the power of the rulers over the people.

Constraints of different kind exist and we are subject to them in different situations. Constraints on freedom can also result from social inequality of the kind implicit in the caste system, or result from extreme economic inequality in a society.

Yes, the constraints are necessary for enjoying freedom because

- It is essential for the creation of a peaceful society.
- It develops respect for differences of views, opinions and beliefs.
- It is required to control violence and settle disputes.

5. Immanuel Kant has argued that human beings possesses dignity. If all persons are granted dignity, then they will have equal opportunity to develop their talents and pursue their chosen goals. The two postulates of Justice are as follow

Truth Truth is the basic postulate of justice. It means exact presentation of an incident. Justice demands objectively that we should be truthful in relating facts concerned with subject-matter.

Equality before Law All the citizens should be equal before law. The citizens should not be discriminated in the name of colour, caste, creed and sex. They should be provided equal opportunities for progress.

6. Different dimensions of Justice helps in creating a just society. Legal, social, political and economic justice are the key dimensions of justice. Economic and Legal Justice are given below

Economic Justice It means to provide equal opportunities to everyone to earn her/his livelihood. It also means to help such people who are not able to work and earn their livelihood. The basic need of every person such as food, cloth, shelter and education should be fulfilled. It stands for by assuring adequate means of livelihood to all, by making provisions for equal pay for equal work, fair distribution of resources, equal economic opportunity to all, etc. While the concept of political justice is closely linked with the ideal of 'liberty', economic and legal justice with 'equality' and social justice with 'fraternity', a just combination of all these four dimensions will help in achieving justice in life.

Legal Justice It is a narrow concept of justice which is associated with the legal system and legal procedure existing in a society. The court of law interprets the law and applies it after hearing the partners involved in a dispute. Here, justice is what administered by the court of law and the interpretation of the judge is considered to be an embodiment of justice.

Or Liberal Theory of Justice is based on three basic principles that are liberty, equality and fraternity. Liberal concept is in fact a legal concept of justice, which is fundamentally based on the rule of law.

Liberal interpretation of justice is quite flexible and emphasises on impartial and independent judiciary. However, Marxian concept of justice is based on economic struggle, which is going on between the rich and the poor.

According to Marxian theory of justice, justice is not possible in the present capitalist state, which is based on force and false consent of the people.

Justice can be established only by abolishing the capitalist state. The dictatorship of proletariat will lead to the establishment of a just society. In fact, justice (just society) will be established when there will be classless and stateless society. Instead of independent judiciary Marxist believe in committed judiciary.

Long Answer Type Questions

7. The Constitution is supreme in our country. The Constitution gives birth to the Indian Parliament. It is the most powerful organisation in the world. The Parliament's influence and prestige have grown as a result of the Parliamentary system of government. Parliament is the people's representative. It has deliberative functions and shapes public opinion through

informative debate and discussion. Parliament is referred to as the people's soul.

Parliament exerts authority over the executive through a variety of means, including the ones listed below.

- Deliberations and debate on the government's policies
- Approval of the Laws Refusal.
- Financial oversight of the executive's motion of no confidence in the government

Every act of omission and commission by the executive is accountable to Parliament. Through Parliament, they are held accountable to the people. Without Parliament's consent, the government is unable to make any expenditures. By impeachment, Parliament can remove the President, Vice President, and judges from their positions. Without the assent of the Indian Parliament within a certain time frame, the executive order of declaration of emergency cannot endure long.

Parliament's authority and reputation have declined throughout the years. The number of Parliamentary sittings has been lowered. Unpleasant sums have poisoned the environment of the Parliament. There is a back-and-forth exchange of allegations and counter-allegations. People with criminal records have been elected to Parliament as a result of the criminalisation of politics. The commercialisation of politics has tainted the mood in the House of Commons.

Due to frequent disruptions, a significant amount of important time in parliament is lost, for which the public must pay. The seriousness with which the house does its business is likewise declining. There is little doubt that the absence of a quorum, as well as a boycott of sessions by opposition members, has made it impossible for the house to exercise oversight over the executive through debate.

Or The powers and functions of the Parliament are as follows

- **Legislative Function** The Parliament is the chief law making body in the country and often merely approves legislations. The task of drafting the bill is done by the bureaucracy under the supervision of the minister concerned. The substance and timing of the bill are decided by the cabinet and no major bill is introduced in the Parliament without the approval of the cabinet.
- **Control of Executive and Ensuring its Accountability** The most vital function of the Parliament is to ensure that the executive does not overstep its authority and remains responsible to the people who have elected them.
- **Financial Function** In a democracy, legislature controls the taxation and its use by the government. No new tax can be introduced without the approval of Lok Sabha. The financial powers of the Parliament involves the grant of resources to the government to implement its programmes. The government has to

give an account to the legislature about the expenditure and resources. In order to ensure that the government does not overspend, the budget and annual financial statements are prepared.

- **Representation** Parliament represent the divergent views of members from different regional, social, economic and religious groups of different parts of the country.
- **Debating Function** The Parliament is the highest forum of debate in the country without any limitation on its power of discussion and the members are free to speak on any matter without fear. These discussions constitute the heart of democratic decision making.
- **Constituent Function** The Parliament has the power to enact changes to the constitution and both the houses are similar in constituent powers. All the amendments have to be approved by a special majority of both the houses of Parliament.

8. **Parliamentary System** The system in which the formulation of policies and enactment of the laws are done by the Parliament is called parliamentary System. In this system, the Prime Minister is the real head of the Government, while the President or Monarch is the nominal head of the state. For example, UK, Portugal, etc opted for parliamentary form of government.

Semi-Presidential System This is the form of government which has both the President and Prime-Minister, where the President is the head of the state and Prime Minister is head of the government, with his council responsible to the legislature. But, unlike the parliamentary system, the President may possess significant day-to-day powers. It is possible that the President and Prime Minister belong to the same party and at times belong to different parties. For example, Russia, Sri Lanka, etc. opted for Semi-Presidential form of government.

The Constituent Assembly debated whether to adopt a Parliamentary or Presidential system of government. Some members supported the Parliamentary system, while others supported the Presidential system, but the ultimate decision was made in favour of the Parliamentary system because we had already run a Parliamentary system under the Government of India Act 1919 and 1935.

This experience shown that the legislative effectively controls the executive in the Parliamentary system. The framers of the Indian Constitution desired a responsible and responsive government that could be held accountable to the people and satisfy their needs. The parliamentary system provides an effective tool for the people through the Parliamentary system to check the executive.

9. "No idea is completely false. What appears to us as false has an element of truth." This statement can be justified in following ways

- JS Mill says that no idea in this world is false. For example, if your parents tell you to become a doctor, engineer or lawyer, etc they are not wrong because they know that it will brighten your future prospects. But if you do not want to go for such career options, then you are also not wrong because you are having interest in some other areas and you think you can brighten your future prospects there. So, nobody is false and nobody is at fault.

- Truth does not emerge by itself. It is only through debates and discussion that truth emerges. Discussion between parents and a young child can lead to the conclusion that the child will go for higher studies. In this way, a child will be able to follow his passion in his area of interest and he will also follow his parents dream of going for higher studies.

- We cannot be sure that the ideas which we considered true is actually true. Ideas which were true at one point of time are false at another point of time. The society that completely suppresses the idea is not acceptable today, and it runs the danger of losing very valuable knowledge.

Or Liberalism is a political ideology which forwards the idea that individuals are naturally endowed with reason and as such be allowed to enjoy the maximum possible freedom.

Liberalism is associated with freedom in the following ways Liberalism and Freedom to Choose Life Partner Modern liberalism focuses on individual. It emphasises on individual's choices and interests. Only individuals are valuable for their choices, e.g., in terms of marriage, only the individuals have full freedom to choose his/ her life partner. Parents or community play only formal role. Liberals give priority to individual's liberty rather than equality. Minimum Administrative Control on Freedom Classical liberalism used to focus on minimal state control where state has only few roles to play as maintaining law and order. Now, liberal state calls for welfare state where the individual is allowed to pursue its own activities but at the same time state take measures to reduce social and economic inequalities.

For Subhash Chandra Bose freedom means all round freedom i.e. freedom for the individual as well as for society; freedom for the rich as well as for the poor; freedom for men as well as for women; freedom for all individuals and for all classes. For him, freedom implies not only liberation from political bondage but also equal distribution of wealth, abolition of caste barriers and social inequities and destruction of communalism and religious intolerance.

10. Feminism is a prominent political theory from the twentieth century that aims to propagate the message of female empowerment. It teaches that men and women are equal in terms of skill and talent capacities. As a result, women should be treated equally and given their proper place in society and decision-making processes at all levels. Many of the inequities that we witness between men and women, according to feminists, are not natural nor necessary. These can be eliminated if we treat men and women equally and allow them to live free lives. Feminism is a powerful worldview that fights for chances for women in all sectors of life, including basic education and increased job prospects for women.

It aims to end patriarchal authority's domination in households and society. Feminists attempt to cast doubt on classical thought. They argue that the biological differences between men and women dictate men's and women's social roles. The feminist movement has played an important part in restoring women's dignity in society and allowing them to demonstrate their importance in various aspects of national life.

Or Socialism is a social system in which each member of the community has an equal part of the many aspects of resource creation, distribution, and trade. A democratic style of governance allows for this type of ownership to exist. A cooperative structure, in which each society member owns a part of shared resources, has also been used to demonstrate socialism.

Socialism is a socio-economic theory that gained popularity in the early twentieth century. It also rejects the disparities that characterised capitalism, which was characterised by a two-class exploitative system. Socialism gained popularity not only in Asian, African, and Latin American emerging countries, but also in European ones. In fact, socialistic thinking for a more equitable society evolved from communist ideology. India's socialist philosophers, such as Ram Manohar Lohiya and Jaiprakash Narayan, highlighted five types of inequities that must be addressed right away. Gender disparities, colour inequalities, caste-based inequalities, and colonialism-based inequalities are all examples of these.

Socialists require that each person be treated according to his or her abilities and that each person be treated according to his or her needs.

Practice Paper 2*
(Unsolved)

General Instructions

■ **Time :** 2 Hours
■ **Max. Marks :** 40

1. There are 10 questions in the question paper. All questions are compulsory.
2. Question no. 1 is a Case Based Question, which has five MCQs. Each question carries 1 mark.
3. Question no. 2-6 are Short Type Questions. Each question carries 3 marks.
4. Question no. 7-10 are Long Answer Type Questions. Each question carries 5 marks.
5. There is no overall choice. However, internal choice have been provided in some questions. Students have to attempt only on of the alternatives in such questions

**** As exact Blue-print and Pattern for CBSE Term II exams is not released yet. So the pattern of this paper is designed by the author on the basis of trend of past CBSE Papers. Students are advised not to consider the pattern of this paper as official. It is just for practice purpose.***

Case Based MCQs

1. Read the given passage and answer the following questions.

Equal treatment is not the only principle of justice. There could be circumstances in which we might feel that treating everybody equally would be unjust…. it would be more fair if students were awarded marks according to the quality of their answer papers and also, possibly, the degree of effort they had put in. In other words, provided everybody starts from the same base line of equal rights, justice in such cases would mean rewarding people in proportion to the scale and quality of their effort. Most people would agree that although people should get the same reward for the same work, it would be fair and just to reward different kinds of work differently if we take into account factors such as the effort required, the skills required, the possible dangers involved in that work, and so on…. For instance, miners, skilled craftsmen, or people in sometimes dangerous but socially useful professions like policemen, may not always get a reward which is just if we compare it to what some others in society may be earning. For justice in society, the principle of equal treatment needs to be balanced with the principle of proportionality. $(5 \times 1 = 5)$

(i) The above passage mentioned about?

   (a) Proportionate Justice   (b) Social Justice

   (c) Restorative Justice   (d) None of these

(ii) The ………… must be reconciled with the principle of equal treatment.

   (a) basic structure   (b) principle of proportionality

   (c) seperation of power   (d) checks and balance

(iii) Which Article of the Indian Constitution deals with the power to review judgement made by the apex court?

   (a) Article 137   (b) Article 131

   (c) Article 147   (d) Article 138

(iv) The Supreme Court's decisions are ………… by all Indian courts.
    (a) enforceable   (b) not enforceble
    (c) separate   (d) Both (a) and (c)

(v) Consider the following statements:
    1. The Supreme Court, is bound to provide advice on such matter as reffered by the President.
    2. The President is not obligated to take such advice as reffered by the Supreme Court.

    Select the correct statement(s)?
    (a) Only 1   (b) Only 2
    (c) Both (1) and (2)   (d) None of these

Short Answer Type Questions

2. Who presides over the meetings of the Joint Sitting of the House? When the President called for the joint session of two House?   **3 Marks**

Or

Which are the areas in which Rajya Sabha has equal powers?

3. What is the procedure to appoint the Prime Minister of India?   **3 Marks**

Or

Compare the powers and position of President of India with the powers and position of the President of United States?

4. What constitutes the electoral college? How does President elects by the electoral college?   **3 Marks**

Or

Why is Keshvananda Bharti Case 1973 significant? What constitutes the doctrine of basic structure?

5. What does the Article 13 of the Indian Constitution says? The concept of Judicial Activism has affect the functioning of Indian Parliament. Explain   **3 Marks**

6. What is the Marx's theory on equality?   **3 Marks**

Long Answer Type Questions

7. What are Parliamentary Secretary? Discuss the role of Parliamentary Secretary in India?   **5 Marks**

Or

What are instruments of Parliamentary control? Discuss briefly.

8. Which type of Executive is based on individual leadership? Briefly explains its sailent features?   **5 Marks**

Or

Discuss the increasing role of Executive in the modern state?

9. Write two aspects of positive liberty. "Eternal vigilance is the price of Liberty". Explain?   **5 Marks**

Or

Define Liberty and explain with examples any three types of Liberty.

10. Explain affirmative action in the context of the Indian Constitution's goal of establishing an equalitarian society.   **5 Marks**

Practice Paper 3* (Unsolved)

General Instructions

- Time : 2 Hours
- Max. Marks : 40

1. There are 10 questions in the question paper. All questions are compulsory.
2. Question no. 1 is a Case Based Question, which has five MCQs. Each question carries 1 mark.
3. Question no. 2-6 are Short Type Questions. Each question carries 3 marks.
4. Question no. 7-10 are Long Answer Type Questions. Each question carries 5 marks.
5. There is no overall choice. However, internal choice have been provided in some questions. Students have to attempt only on of the alternatives in such questions

As exact Blue-print and Pattern for CBSE Term II exams is not released yet. So the pattern of this paper is designed by the author on the basis of trend of past CBSE Papers. Students are advised not to consider the pattern of this paper as official. It is just for practice purpose.

Case Based MCQs

1. Read the given passage and answer the following given questions.

The position of Parliamentary Secretary is one of the highest-ranking government positions. The Parliamentary Secretaries are appointed by India's Prime Minister. Their primary responsibility is to assist cabinet ministers and even the Prime Minister. A Parliamentary Secretary is also responsible for a variety of departmental and parliamentary functions. They work closely with Cabinet Ministers and are also responsible for department-related public and house duties. The Parliamentary Secretary in the House serves as a point of contact for ministers, senators and other members of the House. They contribute to the development of relationships within the government committee. They also have an important role to play in the company of the cabinet members. In the absence of a minister, they will be kept responsible for answering policy questions in the House. (5×1 = 5)

(i) Who appoints Parliamentary Secretaries in India?
   (a) President
   (b) Speaker of the People of House
   (c) Chairman of the Council of State
   (d) Prime Minister

(ii) What is the function of the Parliamentary Secretaries?
   (a) To assist the speaker and chairman of the Parliament.
   (b) To assist the member of parliament who is in opposition.
   (c) To assist cabinet ministers and even the Prime Minister.
   (d) To assist the President of India.

(iii) Parliamentary Secretaries are responsible for answering policy questions in the House if .... is not in the House.
   (a) A minister
   (a) Speaker of the House
   (b) Leader of opposition
   (c) None of these

(iv) A Parliament Secretary often holds the rank of .... and has the same entitlements and is assigned to a government department.

(a) Minister of State   (b) Cabinet Minister
(c) Secretary   (d) None of these

(v) Consider the following statements about Parliamentary secretaries.

1. Parliamentary Secretary helps other ministers in their Parliamentary work.

2. Appointing Parliamentary Secretaries is being seen as an attempt to bypass the cap on number of Council of Ministers.

Which of the following is/are true?

(a) Only 1   (b) Only 2
(c) Both 1 and 2   (d) Neither 1 nor 2

Short Answer Type Questions

2. What are Parliamentary Official? What is the procedure laid down in the constitution for the removal of the Chairman of the Rajya Sabha?   **3 Marks**

Or

How a bill becomes an Act?

3. What constitutes the electoral college? How does President elects by the electoral college?   **3 Marks**

Or

How has the rise of coalition governments since 1989 affected the working of Parliamentary executive?

4. What constitutes the electoral college? How does President elects by the electoral college?   **3 Marks**

Or

What is the procedure for the appointment and removal of the Judges in India?

5. What is Judicial Review? Explain with the help of examples.   **3 Marks**

6. How can we promote Equality? Mention any two methods?   **3 Marks**

Long Answer Type Questions

7. What is a bicameral legislature? Name the states which have bicameral legislation? What are the advantages and disadvantages in favour of the bicameral legislature?   **5 Marks**

Or

Can Rajya Sabha rejects the Money Bill? What is the provision for the joint sitting in the case of Money Bill? Differentiate between Ordinary bill and a Money bill.

8. What is All India Service? How the members of All India Services is elected? Write down function of the UPSC.   **5 Marks**

Or

What is permanent executive? Describe the role of Civil Service in Administration?

9. Examine how the meaning of the word 'freedom' has evolved over time? What kind of societal impact has it had?   **5 Marks**

Or

Explain JS Mill's rationale for freedom of expression.

10. Peace can be best realised where there is freedom, equality and justice ? Do you agree?   **5 Marks**

Printed by Libri Plureos GmbH in Hamburg,
Germany